NATIONAL GEOGRAPHIC KiDS

NOT-SO-COMMON CENT$

SARAH WASSNER FLYNN

NATIONAL GEOGRAPHIC
WASHINGTON, D.C.

CONTENTS

Foreword 6
Introduction 8

CHAPTER 1: A RICH HISTORY 10

All About Bartering 12
Hot Commodities. 16
Big Money 18
Mighty Metals 20
Changes in Change 22
Cashing In 24
Famous Financial Firsts 26

CHAPTER 2: KEEP THE CHANGE 28

Mint Condition 30
Face Off 32
Major Mints Across the Globe 34
Rare Change 36
Striking It Rich 38

CHAPTER 3: FITTING THE BILL 40

Creating Cash. 42
Secret Symbols in the
    $1 Bill Revealed! 44
Cool Cash. 46
The Gold Standard 48
Money Mystery:
    Counterfeit Cash! 50
Counterfeit Criminals Busted! . . 52

CHAPTER 4: SPEND IT, SAVE IT, EARN IT! 54

Bank On It 56
The Business of Banking 58
Extra Credit 60
Grow Your Money 62
Breaking Down
    the Stock Market. 64
Going Broke 66

CHAPTER 5: MONEY AROUND THE WORLD 68

Rich Lands 70
The World's Richest
    Countries 72
The Exchange Rate
    Explained 74
Currency on Every
    Continent. 76
Instant Millions 78
The Culture of Money 80
The Global Effort 82
Not-So-Basic Banks 84

CHAPTER 6:
THE FUTURE OF MONEY 86

- Smarter Cards 88
- Price Check! 90
- Bitcoins and Beyond 92
- Cashing Out 94
- Cool Invention$ 96
- A Look Ahead 98
- Out of This World 100

CHAPTER 7:
WORKING IT!   102

- You're Hired 104
- Five Fast Facts About
     Minimum Wage 106
- Who Makes What? 108
- Famous First Jobs 110
- Changemakers 112
- Whiz Kids! 114
- Odd Jobs 116
- Wild Million-Dollar Ideas! . . 118

CHAPTER 8: START
THINKING MONEY-WISE!   120

- Save It! 122
- Savings Hacks 124
- The Ins and Outs
     of Allowance 126
- Make a Monthly Budget! . . . 128
- Savings Challenges: Show Me
     the Money! 130
- Make That Money! 132

CHAPTER 9:
MORE MONEY FUN!   134

- They Spend What? 136
- Pet Spending
     by the Numbers 138
- Money Myths Busted 140
- Weird but True Facts
     About Money 142
- Paying It Forward 144
- Money Savings Challenge! 146
- Money Quiz:
     Stump Your Parents 148

- Glossary 150
- Index 152
- Photo Credits 158

FOREWORD

A rare 1969 penny **SOLD** for $24,000.

The **FIRST COINS** were bronze, not gold or silver.

The British pound is the **OLDEST** continually used currency in the world.

There are **EIGHT FEATURES** on the U.S. dollar that represent the original 13 Colonies.

There are 54 different countries in Africa—and 15 of them use the **SAME CURRENCY!**

The **LARGEST** denomination ever is a 100,000 peso note issued in the Philippines.

These are all fun facts about money. But learning about money can be practical, too. Money fascinates almost everyone and in many different ways. As we grow up, that fascination usually changes from accumulating fun facts to accumulating actual money. This shift generally occurs when we start earning money—usually as an allowance or from doing chores. Understandably, our first desire is to spend: We want to use the money we've accumulated to get something we want badly—anything from a trendy item of clothing or the newest computer game. How satisfying is that!

As we develop, we begin to see and feel that money is also associated with other desires and ambitions as well as a sense of well-being in life. Budgeting, saving, and then investing become priorities.

Here's the first secret I will share with you: You don't have to understand everything about money at one time. You can learn whatever money-related topic or strategy that is important in your life when you need to or when you are curious about it. Like putting money in a savings account, this knowledge is cumulative, making you smarter at each stage.

Here's the second secret: The more comfortable you are with money and the more you understand that your self-control is part of bringing out the magic in money, you will be able to do good things for yourself and others with the knowledge you continually accumulate.

This book, *Not-So-Common Cents,* is an entertaining, practical place to learn about the fun and serious sides of money. At the same time, you'll acquire important information that will help you make your money work smarter for you during each phase of your life. You can do it!

Alvin Hall

Author of the award-winning children's book *Show Me the Money*

INTRODUCTION

It's true that money isn't everything. But just about everything requires money! No matter where you live, where you go to school, whether you're super into sports or more passionate about art, money is somehow involved in your day-to-day activities. The food you eat, the clothes on your back, the home you live in—they all cost money. And while statistics show you don't need tons of money to make you happy, having a certain amount is correlated with increased happiness—basically enough to live comfortably plus a little extra. Money is a universal language that is spoken in all corners of the Earth ... it indeed makes the world go 'round.

That's why we want you to know everything there is to know about it. From the rich history of money to the coolest currencies you may encounter someday on your globe-trotting adventures, this book will give you a broad look at everything from cash to coins, credit cards to cryptocurrency—and so much

more. Find out how money is made, how banks began, why the cost of certain things changes over time and varies around the world, the very cool ways some people have earned big bucks, and how others share their savings to help people in need.

Most important? This book will get you thinking about how to save smart, spend wisely, and even how to start making your own money ... soon! We hope that being savvy about spending and saving will become your superpower and that by the time you're an adult you'll be a total money pro.

Why is it important to become financially independent? There are so many reasons, but here's a big one: If you're financially independent, not only will you have more choices in life, but you'll also be in a better position to support yourself and others and contribute to your community.

So, dive right in and fill your brain with financial facts! After all, the more you learn, the more you may earn!

And be on the lookout for facts and tips from Chameleonaire!

CHAPTER 1

A RICH HISTORY

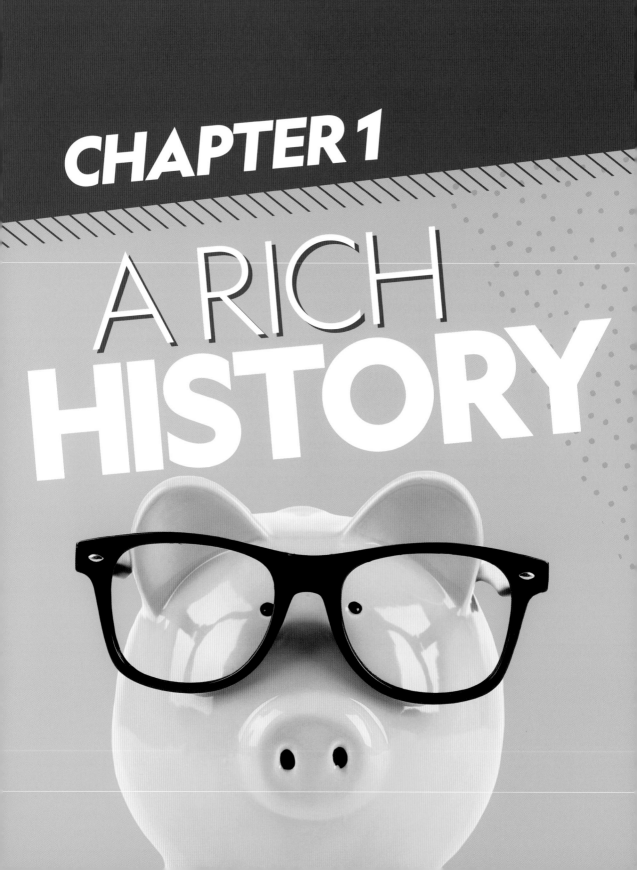

It may be hard to picture a world without money, but it hasn't always been around! Tens of thousands of years ago, people in early civilizations got through life without a cent to their names—literally. They did not know anything about personal wealth, or filling up piggy banks, or even paying for things. For the most part, the earliest known humans lived a much simpler life than we do now, getting by with goods they collected from nature. These included using leaves and animal skins for shelter and clothes, eating animals they hunted and plants they gathered, and making tools from other items such as rocks and wood.

But that all changed when the first known form of currency came on the scene around the sixth or seventh century B.C. (Even before then, people had begun bartering—or trading—tools and food with one another, which ultimately led to the invention of money.) The introduction of money, even in its most basic form, connected people, and it established relationships among those who may not have otherwise interacted. Civilizations were established and enriched as people were able to buy, sell, and trade goods and services that they previously had little access to. Today, money continues to help link people across the planet. But how did we get from trading tools to swiping plastic like we do today? Here's a look at the rich history of money!

ALL ABOUT BARTERING

Picture this: It's close to dinnertime and your parents send you to the store to pick up something to eat. But instead of paying for the food with cash or even a credit card, you give a pair of your mom's earrings to the store's owner! Yep, before currency came about, people offered up their priciest possessions—including animals, jewelry, and other items—in exchange for other valuables. Known as bartering, this type of trading is the earliest known economic transaction—and it's actually still used today.

What is bartering—and how does it differ from trading? Bartering is simply exchanging goods (such as produce) or services (such as labor) without using currency. It is a form of trading—but sometimes, trade can include money, too. So when you barter, you're only passing over a product, not a payment. Which makes sense, since bartering began long before the introduction of currency, like coins or bills. Here's a look at the places and ways people have bartered through the ages.

PREHISTORIC BARTERING

Researchers have traced the beginning of bartering to prehistoric times. While examining artifacts from the cave-dwelling people of Périgord, France, experts found items from not-so-close locations, such as antelope horns from what is modern-day Poland. This likely means that these early humans received the foreign goods through trade with other people passing through the area. What did they offer in return? Perhaps items from their own environment, such as herbs, or special services, such as carving or whittling a tool.

ENTER THE EGYPTIANS

Egyptians were big on bartering—especially as they developed their farming techniques. Beginning around 6000 B.C., farmers would head to markets to trade livestock, such as cows for sheep, or swap grain for oils or vegetables.

BABYLON RULES

Babylon, an ancient city in the region of Mesopotamia, continued to improve on the bartering system. Because Babylonians lacked certain natural resources in their native land, they'd travel to foreign cities to exchange grains, oils, and textiles for timber, wine, and precious metals and stones. At the height of the Babylonian Empire, between the seventh and sixth centuries B.C., you'd find bustling markets where people would travel from near and far to barter products and goods.

SAILING ON

By the ninth century B.C., bartering got a bit more sophisticated as trade routes opened up across the Mediterranean Sea. The Phoenicians, an ancient people who lived in the eastern region of the Mediterranean, established trading routes to the Greek islands, parts of Africa, and parts of Europe, as well as to India and Arabia by crossing the Red Sea. On land, they used caravans to send goods to parts of Asia.

TRIBAL TRADE

Ancient artifacts reveal that Native Americans have been bartering since they first established their civilizations thousands of years ago. Tribes living in different regions would trade with one another to get goods not readily available in their surrounding areas. Items included corn, dried fish, furs, seashells, woven baskets, and resources such as obsidian (a type of rock) to make tools and weapons.

GETTING LUXE IN THE MIDDLE AGES

In the Middle Ages, which lasted from the fifth to the 15th centuries A.D., everyday business was mostly done through barter. Europeans traveled by boat to barter crafts and furs in exchange for luxurious items such as silks and perfumes.

SETTLERS SWAP

Beginning in the 1600s, English colonists arriving in the New World exchanged items such as glass, beads, and copper with Native Americans for their corn. The colonists also swapped services with one another, such as helping a neighbor harvest a crop in exchange for assistance in building a roof on their house.

ANIMALS BARTER, TOO!

>> Humans may be the only species on Earth to exchange currency, but that doesn't mean animals don't wheel and deal, too! Studies show that some species use basic bartering systems when it comes to getting what they want. For example? Chimpanzees in the wild are known to trade services, such as grooming, for food. And a female wasp will offer another wasp exclusive access to her nest in exchange for help raising her offspring. (She'll also boot any bug that doesn't help out enough.) Finally, a study on ravens found that they can be trained to exchange tokens to get their favorite foods—a sign that the clever fliers have an understanding of trade. Who are you calling a birdbrain?

MODERN-DAY BARTERING

By the 18th century, various forms of money were the mainstream way to pay others. But that didn't banish bartering for good. Around the world, people continued to swap services and products without exchanging money. In the 1930s and 1940s, when the economy slumped into the Great Depression, many people returned to bartering. Farmers traded their crops and other goods to those to whom they owed money. Even today, individuals and businesses big and small around the world still practice the art of bartering.

Hair Cut for Stories

Do you wanna share your any stories ?? 👀 ??
(Happy, funny, Sad, angry, scary,

HOT COMMODITIES

Before people exchanged actual money, they made deals by offering up commodities, or valuable objects, which were used as early forms of currency. From salt to squirrels to fake snakes, here's a look at some interesting items traded throughout history!

THE COMMODITY:
COWS

THE DETAILS: Talk about cash cows! Ancient Nubians traded cattle, a sign of wealth and status at the time, with their nearby neighbors the Egyptians for goods such as grain, vegetable oils, and linen.

THE COMMODITY:
COWRIE SHELLS

THE DETAILS: Coastal regions around the Indian Ocean saw the use of these small shells in trade as early as 1200 B.C. Just how much are they worth? In some regions, 500 cowries could be exchanged for a goat!

16

THE COMMODITY:
SQUIRREL PELTS

THE DETAILS: In parts of Europe during the 14th century, squirrel pelts were highly prized items. At one time, a hundred pelts could get you a whole cow.

During the Siberian fur trade of the 17th century, Russians would exchange squirrel pelts as an alternative to sable fur.

THE COMMODITY:
IRON SNAKES

THE DETAILS: The Lobi, an ancient people in today's West Africa, often used iron snakes in trading and bartering. Why? The hand-made replicas, often worn by the Lobi, were believed to protect farmers from real snakes as they worked in the fields.

THE COMMODITY:
SALT

THE DETAILS: In ancient West Africa people often traded salt for gold dust. And in ancient Rome, soldiers were even paid with it. In fact, the word "salary" comes from the Latin word *salarium*, a nod to those Roman soldiers' wages.

THE COMMODITY:
PARMESAN CHEESE

THE DETAILS: In Italy, people have been paying others with Parmesan cheese since the Middle Ages. One Italian bank still accepts wheels of it from clients as loan collateral, which is something offered as part of a promise to repay the money.

A SALTY SALARY

Imagine spending your days risking your life on the battle-field or doing backbreaking work such as building a bridge. And then, at the end of the grueling month, you're handsomely rewarded with ... salt! That's how things were in places like ancient Rome (and later, throughout Europe during the Middle Ages) when salt was a popular form of payment. So what made salt so sought after? At the time, it was super rare! Before the introduction of modern machinery, salt was tough to produce, and even harder to trans-port because of a lack of good roads. Plus, as salt was used to preserve food such as meat, having some extra around meant the soldiers didn't have to hunt for a fresh meal every day. Leftovers, anyone?

17

BIG MONEY

Supersize coins and cash from around the world

Don't bother trying to fit these currencies into your piggy bank!
Here's a look at mega-size money from around the world.

THE CURRENCY: Rai stones
THE LOCATION: The island Yap in the Pacific Ocean
THE SIZE: Some stones weigh as much as a car, stand as tall as an adult, and are wider than a piano.
THE STORY: For hundreds of years, these large limestone disks were used as the main form of payment on Yap. It's believed that as a result of a lack of precious metals or limestone on this tiny Micronesian island, locals traveled to another island to carve the colossal coins out of a mountainside and then hauled them back on rafts.

ALWAYS AND FOREVER

>> Because of their large size, the rai stones actually stayed put in their places on the island. A person would claim a stone as their own or would transfer it to someone else in a public ceremony. And while each village had a stone money "bank"—typically a clearing in the jungle—it didn't really matter where the rai stones were. One legend even tells of a rai stone sinking to the bottom of the ocean during a storm but still being claimed by its owner, since all parties involved agreed that the stone still existed even if they couldn't see it.

Each rai stone has a hole carved into its center, making it slightly lighter and easier to transport on the ocean.

THE CURRENCY: The Australian Kangaroo
THE LOCATION: Perth, Australia
THE SIZE: This commemorative coin weighs more than a buffalo and measures as wide as a microwave.
THE STORY: In 2012, the Perth Mint produced the largest gold coin ever. It features a kangaroo surrounded by sunlight and is made of nearly 100 percent pure gold.

The Australian Kangaroo coin has a face value of nearly a million dollars (U.S.).

THE PERTH MINT
AUSTRALIA

THE CURRENCY: Leather money
THE LOCATION: Ancient China
THE SIZE: One square foot (920 sq cm)
THE STORY: Imagine carting around cash the size of a floor tile! That's what was used in China about 2,100 years ago when people passed around pieces of white deerskin with colorful borders.

Some believe that this type of leather money may be the origins of using "buck" as slang for "dollar."

THE CURRENCY: 100,000 peso note
THE LOCATION: The Philippines
THE SIZE: About the size of a sheet of notebook paper
THE STORY: The world's largest single banknote, this bill was created by the government of the Philippines in 1998 to celebrate the 100th birthday of the Philippine Declaration of Independence, proclaimed on June 12, 1898. It was offered only to collectors for a price tag of some $3,700 (U.S.).

THE CURRENCY: African hoe money
THE LOCATION: Central Africa
THE SIZE: More than two feet (61 cm) tall and nearly one foot (30 cm) across
THE STORY: When metals such as iron, copper, brass, and bronze grew scarce, these heavy tools, typically used in the fields, were used as currency during the 19th and 20th centuries among communities in Central Africa.

People in these regions also exchanged spades, shovels, paddles, and anchors.

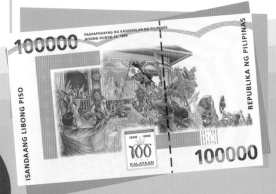

19

MIGHTY METALS

After centuries of bartering, trading, and exchanging objects, the use of actual money became more widely accepted around the sixth century B.C. And, early on in the practice, various civilizations created currency out of precious metals. Here are the glittering details of how metal turned into money.

BRONZE LEADS THE WAY

Around 1100 B.C., people in China began making small replicas of goods, such as knives and shells, cast from bronze. Later, these casts evolved into round coins with square holes in the center, which are considered the first use of standardized currency. The ancient Romans also made the most of the abundance of bronze by trading pieces of it. These bits of bronze eventually evolved into coins.

A SILVER LINING

Used in major empires from ancient Greece and Rome to colonial America, silver is one of the most common forms of currency. In fact, more than 4,000 years ago in ancient Greece, rough-cut bars of silver—also known as ingots—were used in trade. Ancient Greek city-states made silver coins with intricate designs, such as the famous owl and Athena coin that features the goddess of wisdom and warfare on one side and her animal companion on the other. The largest silver coin of its time, it also sparked the trend of two-sided coins—a feature we still see in today's change.

GOOD AS GOLD

The first use of pure gold in coins with stamped images dates back to the sixth century B.C. in Lydia—an ancient kingdom located in modern-day Turkey. Because some gold may also contain silver, the Lydians eventually figured out how to purify their gold by mixing in salt and turning up the heat, which vaporized the silver and left behind nothing but the shiny golden stuff.

20

PRECIOUS METAL

>> There are plenty of metals and other elements on Earth that could potentially be used for currency. So why is gold considered especially, well, precious? Experts say it has to do with science! Unlike many other elements, gold isn't reactive. This means it doesn't burst into flames when exposed to air, as lithium does, or rust when exposed to water, as iron does. Also it's not radioactive, which means it can't hurt you if you keep it close by. Even silver tarnishes, but gold doesn't. Gold also melts at a much lower temperature than, say, platinum, plus it's the most malleable metal, making it much easier to manipulate into a coin—or another form of shiny bling.

CHANGES IN CHANGE

When did currency first come to be in the United States? Actually, creating a currency system was one of the first projects taken on by the U.S. Congress, which ultimately passed the Coinage Act in 1792 that was signed into law by President George Washington. This established the U.S. Mint and regulated coin production. But the system has not remained status quo over the past 230 years. Here's a look at how U.S. change has, well, changed over time.

SMALL CHANGE

What can you buy for half of a cent? Back in the 1800s, perhaps you could pick up a quart of milk or maybe a magazine. Between 1793 and 1857, the U.S. Mint produced the country's smallest denomination, worth just half a penny. For as little as it was worth, the coin was rather large—about the size of a quarter.

RARE BIRDS

These days, most change is made from a mix of metals. But at one point, the U.S. Mint produced special coins made out of pure gold. Known as eagle coins, they were first produced in 1795 and came in denominations of $2.50, $5, and $10. In 1933, in an attempt to save the struggling economy, President Franklin Delano Roosevelt outlawed owning gold bars or gold certificates—and the circulation of gold as well. Anyone who owned these items had to take them to a bank and exchange them for dollars. And if they didn't? They faced a stiff fine of $10,000 (that's about $200,000 in today's dollars!), up to 10 years in prison, or both! The restrictions remained until 1974, when President Gerald Ford finally reversed Roosevelt's decision.

In 2002, a gold eagle coin from 1933 sold at auction for $7.6 million.

22

THREE'S A CHARM

You've probably heard of a silver dollar, but what about a golden three-dollar piece? If you lived in the United States in the late 1800s, you may have had one of these coins in your pocket. While intricately designed—Lady Liberty wearing a Native American princess headdress was etched on one side, with a wreath of corn, wheat, cotton, and tobacco on the other—it wasn't a very popular piece and was mostly used by businesses to buy three dollars worth of stamps in one easy transaction.

Very rare three-dollar coins from 1854 are worth as much as $100,000 today!

James Barton Longacre, who designed the three-dollar piece as well as other early U.S. pieces, would often include a tiny "L" somewhere on the coin as his calling card.

Quarters and dimes may look super shiny, but they actually don't contain a speck of silver! In fact, ever since 1971, no currency circulated by the U.S. Mint (aside from some collectible coins) has been made of silver. And pennies went from mostly copper to mostly zinc in 1982. Why? As the price of precious metals increased over time, the composition of coins changed. Here's a glimpse at what your money is made of!

THE COIN: Penny
THEN: 100% copper
NOW: 2.5% copper, 97.5% zinc

THE COIN: Nickel
THEN: Nearly 100% silver
NOW: 25% nickel, 75% copper

THE COINS: Dimes and quarters
THEN: Nearly 100% silver
NOW: 8.3% nickel, 91.7% copper

THE COIN:
One-dollar piece
THEN:
Nearly 100% silver
NOW: 88.5% copper,
6% zinc, 3.5%
manganese, 2% nickel

MAKE MORE CENTS!

Gather up your loose change and take a closer look to see if you have an old or rare coin hiding in plain sight!

CASHING IN

Bills, bucks, Benjamins ... what do these words have in common? They're all slang for paper money! In the United States, the dollar bill began circulating in 1862, but various forms of cash were used in different parts of the world well before then. Read on for a timeline of how early bills came to be.

Around A.D. 800

After using copper coins for centuries, the Chinese wanted a way to haul around hefty amounts of money without being weighed down. Their solution? Exchanging their coins for much lighter paper certificates—which reflected the value of their coins and could be easily tucked away.

Early Chinese bills were said to be called flying money since they often blew away on windy days.

1290

Explorer Marco Polo travels to China and takes note of their paper money, bringing the concept back to Europe with him (although it would take hundreds of years for the idea to catch on).

1294

Paper money spreads to Persia and, later, to parts of India and Japan. But merchants in these regions aren't big fans of the system, and it ultimately fades away for several hundred years.

1438

A Spanish military leader is said to have paid his soldiers with paper notes after an invasion.

1455

China eliminates paper money and returns to a coin-only currency. The word "cash" is said to be rooted in the Chinese word used to describe their round bronze coins.

1776

The U.S. Continental Congress issues $2 "bills of credit." Printed infrequently these days, the $2 bill is the country's rarest form of currently produced currency.

1861

In order to finance the Civil War, the U.S. Congress authorizes the Department of the Treasury to issue Demand Notes, also called greenbacks because of their color.

1862

The first $1 bill is issued in the United States. It features a portrait of Salmon P. Chase, the secretary of the Treasury under President Abraham Lincoln. Marked with a red seal and serial number, these early bills continued to circulate until they were discontinued in 1971.

1694

The British pound comes on the scene—and stays. To date, it's the longest-running paper currency in the world.

1661

The first banknotes are printed in Sweden. These slips of paper are given to bank customers in exchange for the country's bulkier copper plate money.

FAMOUS
FINANCIAL FIRSTS

Eight major money milestones throughout history

WHAT:
The first modern bank
WHEN: 1472   **WHERE:** Italy
Some 550 years ago, Banca Monte dei Paschi di Siena opened its doors for the first time—and the bank remains open today. During the 17th and 18th centuries, the bank offered Italian citizens the very first mortgage loans (an agreement that allows you to borrow from the bank to buy a home).

WHAT:
The first modern decimal currency
WHEN: 1704   **WHERE:** Russia
In 1704, Tsar Peter the Great introduces the first modern system of decimal currency by making one ruble equal to a hundred kopecks. Later, other countries picked up this system, which is why the U.S. dollar is equal to a hundred pennies.

WHAT:
The first circulating coins in the United States
WHEN: 1793   **WHERE:** Philadelphia, Pennsylvania, U.S.A.
With its initial batch of 11,178 copper pennies, the mint delivered the original U.S. coins. But it took a while: At the time, the mint's coin presses could only produce a few dozen coins a minute.

WHAT: The first credit card
WHEN: 1946 **WHERE:** Brooklyn, New York, U.S.A.
John Biggins, an employee at a bank in Brooklyn, invents the Charg-It card that lets people charge purchases to the bank—as long as they were within a two-square-block radius of the bank.

WHAT: The first transcontinental electronic transfer of money
WHEN: 1871 **WHERE:** The United States
The telegram company Western Union becomes the first to allow customers to wire money from one account to someone else's even if they're thousands of miles away.

WHAT: The first African American to appear on a U.S. coin
WHEN: 1946 **WHERE:** The United States
Booker T. Washington, a former enslaved person who rose to become an admired educator and politician in the early 1900s, is honored with a commemorative half-dollar featuring his face on the front and the quote "From Slave Cabin to Hall of Fame" on the back.

WHAT: The first ATM
WHEN: 1967 **WHERE:** London, England
Inventor John Shepherd-Barron comes up with an automatic teller machine—aka an ATM—that doled out cash from people's bank accounts upon entering a PIN (personal identification number) code.

WHAT: The world's first gold coin with a diamond
WHEN: 2012
WHERE: Canada
To mark Queen Elizabeth's Diamond Jubilee, the Royal Canadian Mint produces a coin crafted in 99.999 percent pure gold, and glittering with a tiny diamond.

CHAPTER 2

KEEP THE
CHANGE

Coins: They're everywhere! Chances are you've got plenty of change lying around your house, from piling up in your junk drawer to filling up your piggy banks. First introduced as a method of payment thousands of years ago, billions and billions of coins are in circulation around the world today. From creating them to collecting them, read on to find out what makes coins so cool!

MINT CONDITION

A LOOK AT HOW MONEY IS MADE

Centuries ago, the job of creating coins was done by individuals who would melt down precious metals and shape them into tokens. But as the process of paying for items and services in regulated currency became more mainstream, there was a demand for facilities that could pump out piles and piles of change. These are known as mints, and they are typically run by a country's government to make sure that the amount of money that's made and then goes out into the world stays in check.

Mint Evolution

While mints have been around for thousands of years—there's evidence of minting dating back to ancient Egypt and Greece!—the process became a lot more efficient after the industrial revolution, when steam-powered machines could create coins at a quicker rate. (Much later, computers sped up the process even more.) In 1792, the U.S. Congress established the country's first national mint in Philadelphia, Pennsylvania, following the footsteps of already established facilities in Europe. Today, there are four active mints in the United States (and many more around the world; flip to page 34 for details!) that collectively produce billions of coins.

MAKING CHANGE

From metal to money: 6 steps to creating coins at a mint

STEP 1: BLANKING

Most coins start off as strips of metal about as long as four American football fields and about as wide as a ruler; these strips are fed into a machine called a blanking press. This machine punches out round disks from the strip called blanks because they are just that: plain tokens. As for the leftover metal? It's shredded and recycled, usually into another sheet of metal.

STEP 2: ANNEALING, WASHING, AND DRYING

The blanks are then annealed, or heated, in a furnace and slowly cooled—a process that softens the metal. They are then run through a washing and drying station.

30

STEP 3: UPSETTING

The blanks go through a mill which "upsets" the coins, or raises a rim around their edges. This creates a planchet—the disk-shaped metal piece that's ready to be pressed.

STEP 4: STRIKING

The planchets are fed through a coining press, which stamps the designs and inscriptions.

STEP 5: INSPECTION

A mint employee known as a press operator carefully spot-checks each batch of new coins using a magnifying glass. If the cents aren't up to snuff? Labeled "mules," these rejected coins are typically tossed or recycled to make more coins (but some escape into circulation—see the sidebar for more!).

STEP 6: COUNTING AND BAGGING

A machine counts the coins and drops them into bags, which are sealed and eventually taken off to banks, where the coins are distributed ... and eventually land in your hands.

INCORRECT CHANGE

It doesn't happen often, but errors on coins can go unnoticed by a mint inspector. And when these flawed pieces go out into circulation, they may actually *increase* in value. Take, for example, a set of super-rare British two-pence coins, which were accidentally printed by the Royal Mint on the base of a nickel-plated 10-pence piece. (All other two-pence coins are made of copper-plated steel.) After one of these error coins was tossed into a charity bin, it was almost thrown away. But a keen-eyed collector recognized its rareness and eventually put it up for auction. The pence's price? About 67,500 times its face value.

And then there's the 2004 Wisconsin State Quarter, some of which were printed with what looks like an extra leaf on the ear of corn etched on the tail side. Coin collectors clamor over these quarters—which can be worth around $100 each. Now *that's* more than just pocket change!

MAKE MORE CENTS!

Have a family member who has oodles of loose change? Offer to collect it and sort it. Look for any errors or interesting features. You just may find something special—and, if you're lucky, they might let you keep it, too!

FACE OFF

STORIES ABOUT THE FAMOUS FACES YOU SEE ON MONEY

From kings and queens to popes and politicians, hundreds of historical and famous figures have been etched into coins around the world. Experts say a Persian nobleman named Tissaphernes—who ruled in the fourth century B.C.—was the first actual human to be featured on a coin, made in the ancient kingdom of Lydia. Before then? Coins were either plain or included images of gods and goddesses. As time passed, ancient Egyptians and Romans began stamping coins with military heroes, royalty, and religious figures—a trend that has continued for centuries around the world.

MONEY MAKEOVER

After the American Colonies gained independence from the British, images of the United States' newfound freedom started popping up on coins, with Lady Liberty and an American eagle showing up first. In 1909, the face of Abraham Lincoln was added to the one-cent piece to mark the 100th anniversary of his birth. And in 1938, an image of Thomas Jefferson was selected in a public art contest and added to the nickel. Soon other coins were created to honor other presidents. However, not just anyone can be featured on a piece of change: Federal law states that no living person can appear on official U.S. coinage, and presidents must be dead for at least two years before they can be considered.

LADIES FIRST

While the United States hasn't had a female president—yet—some remarkable women have made their way onto American coins. They include Virginia Dare, the first child to be born to English colonist parents in the Americas. She is shown as an infant being held by her mother on the back of the 1937 half-dollar, a commemorative coin. Other fierce females who have been forever immortalized on the face of a coin include Helen Keller, women's rights activist Susan B. Anthony, Special Olympics founder Eunice Kennedy Shriver, First Lady Dolley Madison, and Native American Sacagawea.

Cleopatra made sure she appeared alone on ancient Egyptian coins as a way to symbolize her independence and political power.

The coin representing 1/100 of a U.S. dollar is officially called a cent. "Penny" is just a nickname.

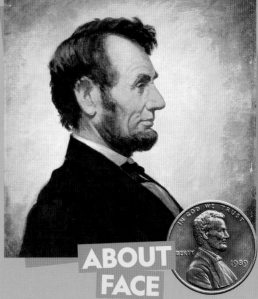

ABOUT FACE

》》 Almost every figure who appears on a modern coin is shown from the side, or in profile. And that decision all has to do with art! Because most coins are pretty small and thin, it's tough to show individual facial features head-on. Profiles, on the other hand, allow an artist to show more distinctive details, such as the nose shape and jawline—even in a supersmall space. And as for which direction those figures face? With American money, almost every person featured on a coin is looking left. (Some experts assess that by facing left they're "looking to past accomplishments.") One exception? Abraham Lincoln on the penny. A portrait that was originally based on a photo of the former president, taken in 1864, showed Lincoln facing right, so he wound up looking the same way on the coin.

33

MAJOR MINTS
ACROSS THE GLOBE

When it comes to making money, these mints stamp out the rest!

THE OLDEST!

WHERE: Paris, France
Founded in 864, La Monnaie de Paris is the longest-standing continuously running mint in the world. It is also considered the oldest enterprise, or business, in France.

THE BIGGEST!

WHERE: Philadelphia, Pennsylvania, U.S.A.
Spreading over an area bigger than three soccer fields, the Philadelphia Mint covers more ground than any other facility of its kind. Since it was established in 1792, the mint has had three locations in the city. The current facility, operating since 1969, produces more than 35 million coins every day.

The term "mint condition"—referring to any item that's in excellent shape—was originally used by collectors to describe the condition of coins.

THE NEWEST!

WHERE: Tarlac, Philippines
The Philippine government is building a brand-new, state-of-the-art mint outside of the capital city of Manila. With plans for a facility set on nearly 80 acres (32 ha), it is also one of the world's biggest mints.

THE SMALLEST!

WHERE: Rome, Italy

This single-press mint located in a small room pumps out coins unique to the Sovereign Military Order of Malta, a neutral, non-political organization focused on social, medical, and humanitarian efforts.

DO ALL COUNTRIES HAVE MINTS?

>> While large countries—such as the United States—need more than one mint to keep up with coin production, others are simply too small or lack the resources to produce their own currency. So they outsource to foreign mints, such as the Bavarian State Mint in Munich, Germany, which provides certain coins to other countries, including Denmark, Greece, and Israel.

THE RECORD SETTER!

WHERE: Perth, Australia

In 2012, the Perth Mint produced the largest pure gold coin ever, the Australian Kangaroo One Tonne Gold Coin, which has a face value of one million Australian dollars!

THE MOST PRODUCTIVE!

WHERE: Winnipeg and Ottawa, Canada

Aside from producing all of Canada's coins, the Royal Canadian Mint, which has two locations, has produced coinage for more than 70 foreign countries, from Algeria to Zambia.

ELIZABETH II · AUSTRALIA · 1000000 DOLLARS

RARE CHANGE

Six of the coolest and most unique coins from around the world!

THE COIN: Paddington Bear 50p
WHY IT'S COOL: In 2019, the United Kingdom's Royal Mint released two designs of a 50-pence piece featuring the fictional, marmalade-loving bear visiting the Tower of London and St. Paul's Cathedral.

THE COIN: Chinese dragon dollar
WHY IT'S COOL: This 1911 coin showcases a long-whiskered dragon, a symbol of power in China, on its front. Über-rare, it's a coveted collector's item; one recently sold for $140,000.

THE COIN: Flowing hair dollar
WHY IT'S COOL: One of the first dollar coins ever minted by the U.S. government, this pricey piece dates back to 1794. Featuring Lady Liberty (and her flowing mane) on the front and an eagle on the back, it sold for $10,016,875 at an auction in 2013, setting a world-record price for *any* coin.

THE COIN: Glow-in-the-dark dinosaur
WHY IT'S COOL: In daylight, this Canadian quarter features the image of a *Pachyrhinosaurus*, a dinosaur whose remains were discovered in the province of Alberta. Take it into a dark room to reveal the dino's glowing skeleton!

THE COIN: "Tara" of Vijayanagar
WHY IT'S COOL: Arguably the world's smallest coin, this bit is small enough to fit on the tip of your pinkie. Hailing from India, the tiny piece was likely issued in the 14th century.

THE COIN: King Tut pyramid
WHY IT'S COOL: The world's first pyramid-shaped coin, this piece was issued by the Isle of Man (a self-governing island located in the Irish Sea between England, Scotland, and Ireland) to celebrate a King Tut museum exhibit in neighboring London.

THE TRUTH ABOUT TENDER

You may have heard the word "tender" to describe money. But what does the term actually mean? Technically, legal tender refers to currency that's been approved by law. It also defines the valid type of payment you can use to repay a debt. So, say you owe your brother 15 bucks. Legally, you can't pay him back in toys worth that amount because toys aren't tender. But you can pay him back with 60 quarters, or 1,500 pennies, because those coins are considered legal tender. But he may not like it!

STRIKING IT RICH

TURNING SMALL CHANGE INTO BIG BUCKS

Can you get rich collecting coins? Maybe! Coin collecting has been a popular pastime for centuries, and some collectors—also called numismatists (new-MIZ-muh-tists)—have struck it rich with rare hauls. One of the most famous coin collectors? Louis E. Eliasberg, a banker from Baltimore, Maryland, U.S.A., who managed to snag every major coin released by the United States. His collection sold for a grand total of $44,900,000 among three sales between 1982 and 1997. Now *that's* some serious coin.

Seeking Change

Aside from seeking complete collections like Eliasberg did, many numismatists are constantly on the lookout for unique coins. Around the world, enthusiasts head to coin conventions or go online in the hopes of finding valuable currency, while "coin roll hunters" pick up rolls of change from banks simply to sift through each one looking for rare bits. In 2017, one woman in Texas, U.S.A., hit the jackpot after discovering a rare 1969 cent among rolls of some 7,500 pennies. The coin—known by collectors as a Doubled Die Obverse cent—features a telltale overlapping of details, the result of a mishap at the mint. And with a value of about $24,000, that makes for one very expensive error!

WHAT MAKES A COIN VALUABLE?

Break out a magnifying glass and check your change!

THERE'S AN ERROR ON IT. ....

Big, noteworthy errors can fetch a pretty penny. Seeing double in the details on your coin? It may be worth a lot!

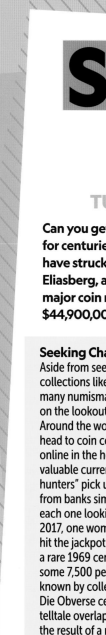

IT'S SUPER RARE.

Limited release coins are valuable simply because there are fewer of them out there. Reading up on rare coins will give you a specific idea of what to look for.

IT'S OLD.

Generally, the older the coin, the more it's worth. Even better if an old coin is in excellent condition with little visible wear.

Once popular among royalty and the very wealthy, coin collecting is still known as the "hobby of kings."

Every year, travelers passing through security at major airports in the United States leave behind some one million dollars in loose change.

IT'S SILVER.

Any dime, quarter, or half-dollar minted before 1965 is made mostly of silver—making it much more valuable than those composed of a less precious metal.

39

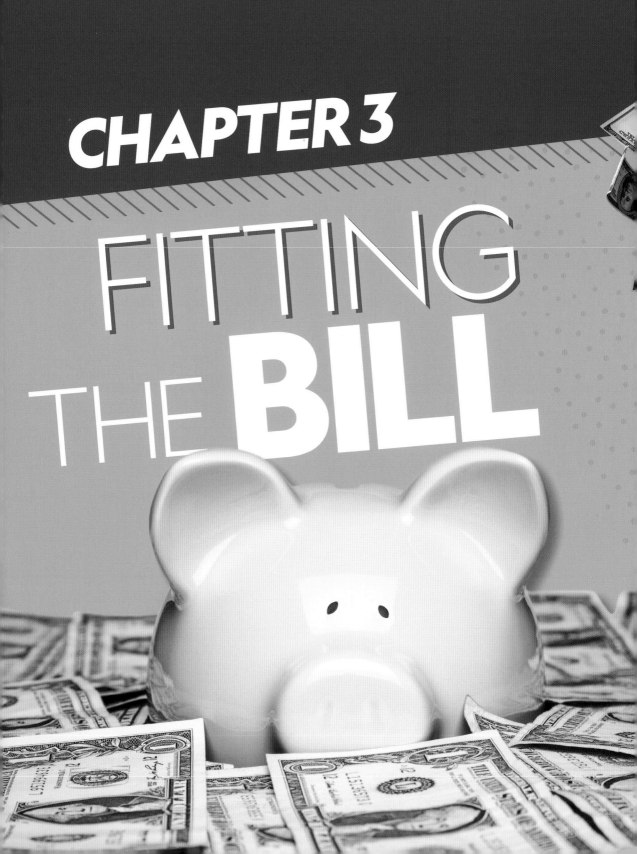

CHAPTER 3

FITTING
THE BILL

Paper money has been around since the days of the ancient Chinese (they exchanged special certificates as big as a piece of notebook paper!), but it took until the 17th century before it really became the norm in Europe, and, later, elsewhere. Today, there are billions of bills circulating around the United States alone, with almost every country producing paper currency of its own. So what's so cool about this kind of currency? Plenty! First, many bills are made from a unique type of paper meant to withstand years of exchange between people. (They can even survive several cycles through a washing machine.) Paper money can also be pretty: Some countries produce brightly colored bills featuring pictures of native animals, famous figures, and even original artwork. There may even be a hidden message or two on your bills if you look hard enough—secret symbols mostly meant to show it's the real deal, and not fake money. Yep, cash is pretty cool. Read on to find out more about paper money!

CREATING CASH

THE BUSINESS OF MAKING BUCKS

If a mint makes coins, what do you call the place that prints paper money? In the United States, it's the Bureau of Engraving and Printing (BEP), with locations in Washington, D.C., and Fort Worth, Texas. Internationally, banknotes are produced in nongovernment facilities, which may print paper money for several countries at once. In fact, only a handful of countries—including the United States and India—make their money on home turf. The rest outsource to foreign facilities. The company De La Rue, in England, designs one-third of all banknotes in circulation around the world.

It's Complicated

The business of making money is fairly complicated because each piece that's produced goes through extensive testing for security and function and is carefully tracked, packaged, and stored in vaults. There's a ton of security surrounding the process to avoid theft as well as the creation of counterfeit money (more on that on page 50!).

In the United States, the process of making money has evolved over the years. Back at the beginning of the BEP in 1862, people used to crank cash through machines by hand and separate notes from sheets using scissors in the basement of the Treasury building. Today, modern technology allows for a precise, sophisticated system that can produce millions of banknotes every month—each of which is inspected by high-tech equipment.

PRODUCING PAPER MONEY

How is paper money made? Here's the process in the United States.

STEP 1:

Banknote designers use traditional drawing tools to create mock-ups of bills before the images are digitized. Once approved, the design is turned into a 3D engraving. Portraits of people on the bill (think Benjamin Franklin and Alexander Hamilton) are engraved on special steel plates through a printmaking process known as intaglio.

STEP 2:

Large pallets of "paper" are loaded into high-speed presses, which can print one side of a bill at a rate of 10,000 sheets an hour. This isn't any ordinary paper, though. All U.S. money is printed on special paper that's 75 percent cotton and 25 percent linen with red and blue fibers woven in. This gives it a much softer feel than regular paper—and it makes it more durable, too.

STEP 3:

The front of the bills (like faces and details including the freedom icons) are printed in black ink. The remaining printing details depend on the bill's denomination: For example, $10, $20, and $50 bills feature a metallic ink in addition to the standard black.

STEP 4:

As the paper passes through the presses, each sheet is carefully tracked and charted. (Every bill has a combo of 11 numbers and letters [or 10 for currency printed before 1966] that appears twice on the front.)

STEP 5:

After printing, the sheets are separated and dry for at least 72 hours before the process is repeated and the other side is printed. Then the currency sheets are cut into single notes and packaged for shipping to the Federal Reserve.

STEP 6:

The printed sheets are inspected by high-speed technical equipment. If approved, they're cut into bill shapes, packed up, and shipped out.

In the United States, there are more $100 bills in circulation than $1 bills.

WHERE DOES NEW MONEY GO?

Brand-new bills are sent from the BEP to the Federal Reserve, the central bank of the United States, and placed in a vault. Eventually, the money is distributed to Federal Reserve Banks, then to smaller banks, after which it ends up in stores (and in people's wallets).

SECRET INK

Have you ever accidentally left a dollar in, say, the pocket of your pants—which then winds up in the laundry? When you fish it out of the dryer, the dollar bill may be a bit crumpled or flat as a result, but the color remains mostly the same. That's because each dollar bill is printed in a special permanent ink blended especially by the BEP that's hard to wash away. The formula of the ink is actually top secret, to avoid clueing in potential counterfeiters.

SECRET SYMBOLS
IN THE $1 BILL
REVEALED!

When it comes to the details of the U.S. dollar bill, there's so much more than meets the eye.

A GREAT PYRAMID

A pyramid may be a peculiar addition to an American dollar bill, but it represents a lot more than just an ancient Egyptian monument. The 13 steps on the pyramid are symbolic of the original Colonies. It's unfinished to show the newness of the country, as well as the strength and duration of the United States.

EYE SPY

What's up with the eye above the pyramid? Experts theorize that it means an "all-seeing God" that is looking after the country.

As for the letters at its base? MDCCLXXVI is the Roman numeral for 1776, the year the United States was established.

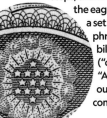

CUTE CRITTER

Whoooo is that? Take a peek at the top right corner of the dollar bill above the "1" and you'll spot a tiny critter hanging out in the notch design. Some people think it's an owl, meant to represent Minerva, the goddess of wisdom. Another theory? It's a spider in a web—but no one is quite sure about the possible arachnid's potential origins.

LUCKY 13

Who says 13 is unlucky? When the Founding Fathers designed the look of the dollar bill, they made sure to represent the original 13 Colonies in various symbols. The arrows in the eagle's talons, the olive branch leaves, the berries on the olive branch, the stars above the eagle, the pyramid steps, and the bars on the shield on the eagle's chest all appear in a set of 13. Even the Latin phrases featured on the bill, "E Pluribus Unum" ("one of many") and "Annuit Cœptis" ("favors our undertakings") are composed of 13 letters.

SEAL IT

The Great Seal on the back of the dollar includes an eagle that is a nod to the Founding Fathers' mantra that the United States has "a strong desire for peace, but will always be ready for war." The olive branch in the eagle's talons is a symbol of peace, while the arrows it holds on the other side are representative of war.

MAKE MORE CENTS!

Is your bill worth more than a buck? Check the serial number! Each dollar bill has a serial number printed on it, which is how the BEP keeps track of each note. And some collectors will pay big money for bills with certain serial numbers. Those that are considered the luckiest? Serial numbers that have seven of the same digits in a row (like 88888880), "double quads" (like 99990000), and digits that have patterns of just two numbers (like 00090000 or 00101000). Some collectors have paid up to $5,000 for a single dollar bill featuring a super-rare serial number. Now that's one way to get rich quick!

COOL CASH

Seven wacky and wonderful bills from around the world

Australia's cash is coated with polymer, which is a waxy, waterproof plastic.

Queen Elizabeth II's portrait has been on the currencies of at least 35 different countries—more than any other person.

BUMPY BILL
WHAT: Australia's banknotes
WHY IT'S COOL: Bills from down under have two little raised dots to help those with impaired vision to identify the currency.

GREAT GOLD
WHAT: China's 100-yuan bill
WHY IT'S COOL: The gold numbers on this bill aren't just there for a glittery touch: The shiny hue is actually harder to forge.

In 2019, an anonymous donor left a $1,000 bill in a Salvation Army charity kettle.

A VERY GRAND BILL
WHAT: U.S. $1,000 bill
WHY IT'S COOL: Up until 1945, the United States printed this big bill featuring President Grover Cleveland. They were pulled from circulation by the government in 1969, but those that are still floating around may be worth several times their face value.

COLORFUL CASH
WHAT: Costa Rican colons
WHY IT'S COOL: This cash is covered with exotic animals that call the country home, such as sloths, hummingbirds, monkeys, and butterflies.

BEAUTIFUL BANKNOTES
WHAT: Icelandic krona
WHY IT'S COOL: The country's bills feature detailed images of historical Icelandic characters, famous artists, and reprints of paintings.

NUMBER GAME
WHAT: Zimbabwean 100-trillion-dollar bill
WHY IT'S COOL: This bill featured the most zeros of any legal tender in all recorded history. It's no longer printed and is simply used as a collector's item these days.

WILD BUCKS
WHAT: South African rand
WHY IT'S COOL: South Africa's banknotes feature some of the standout animals that call the country home: a rhinoceros, elephant, lion, buffalo, and leopard.

Which country has the coolest-looking cash? That's a title decided by the International Bank Note Society in their annual Bank Note of the Year competition. Governments from across the world submit their brand-new designs for the contest, and the winners are chosen based on elements such as artwork and innovative security features. Some of the recent winners? The purple-hued Canadian $10 bill featuring civil rights activist Viola Desmond—the first Canadian woman to be featured prominently on a bill—as well as the Mexican 100-peso note with a portrait of poet Sor Juana Inés de la Cruz—one of the country's national heroines—and monarch butterflies on the back.

THE GOLD STANDARD

WHEN WE RUN OUT OF MONEY, WHY CAN'T WE JUST PRINT MORE?

s there such a thing as too much money? Yes—at least when it comes to printing it. In fact, back when some countries first started their systems of paper currency, they ran into a big problem: They created way more money than they could keep up with or redeem. And the more bills that were made, the less they were worth. This decrease in value is also known as inflation—and it made the exchange of money for goods and services very complicated. Suddenly, that money was worth a heck of a lot less than it was worth before.

GOLD STANDARD GOES GLOBAL

The solution? The Gold Standard, which several countries, including the United States, adopted for the better part of the 19th and 20th centuries. This monetary system tied the value of a country's currency to gold. In other words, someone could potentially take their cash into a bank and redeem it for a specific amount of gold—an amount that was regulated around the world. That way, a country could not increase the amount of money in circulation without also increasing its gold reserves. And that meant a lot of gold. The United States, for example, held $19.4 billion in gold reserves in 1960—enough to cover all of its bills floating around the world.

A NEW SYSTEM

The Gold Standard held mostly strong for decades, eventually falling out of fashion with the United States and being replaced with fiat currency, a system that places paper money's value on the strength of the government that issues it, not its worth in gold or silver. It's like a promise from a government or central bank that says "Your dollar bill has value," and it is based on the idea that people all agree that money is worth a certain amount.

MORE MONEY, MORE PROBLEMS

That's not to say countries haven't tried to print more money to pay off debts and boost their economy. But as more bills are circulated, their values decrease and so prices go way up. This results in hyperinflation, which means prices rapidly increase. In 2008, when Zimbabwe printed extra cash, their prices rose by as much as 231,000,000 percent in a single year! To put that into perspective, a single loaf of bread cost 10 million Zimbabwe dollars. That's a lot of bills for bread!

The bottom line? If a government prints more money than it can support, prices will undoubtedly rise. And that's a system that's just not sustainable for the long term.

WHO'S GOT THE GOLD?

≫ So what happened to all of the gold once the standard fell out of fashion? It's still around. In fact, most big banks still hold gold reserves to protect against hyperinflation or other economic catastrophes. Almost every country has some gold stored up, with the United States leading the charge with a stockpile of gold weighing more than 435 whale sharks!

United States: 8,965 tons (8,133 t)

Germany: 3,705 tons (3,361 t)

Italy: 2,703 tons (2,452 t)

France: 2,685 tons (2,436 t)

Russia: 2,530 tons (2,295 t)

10,000
8,000
6,000
4,000
2,000
0

Some four billion years ago, meteor showers—the result of collisions between dead stars—rained gold down on Earth.

49

MONEY MYSTERY: COUNTERFEIT CASH!

WHY MAKING FAKE MONEY IS A REAL CRIME

For centuries, counterfeit money has proved to be a major problem around the world. Simply put, counterfeit money is printed to look like the real deal—only it has no value. And anyone who unknowingly takes fake money in exchange for a product or service is left with zilch. As a result, the act of forging money is considered a serious crime: People busted for counterfeiting can be fined and sent to prison for up to 20 years.

ALL ABOUT BENJAMIN

People have been producing fake money practically since paper currency came about. In the mid-1700s, Benjamin Franklin was the first person to address the issue of counterfeiting when he took on the job as the official money printer for the state of New Jersey. A keen inventor, Franklin came up with ways to prove the bills he produced were legit. His approach? Making stamps with individual leaves that he inked onto the backs of the bills. (Franklin figured that counterfeiters would have trouble reproducing the unique design.) On some bills, he even deliberately misspelled the word "Pennsylvania." His reasoning was that a forger would miss that detail and use the *correct* spelling on any note they created—making it easier to spot a fake. Sneaky!

CRACKING DOWN ON COUNTERFEIT

Despite Franklin's attempts, counterfeit money remained a giant problem in the United States for years to come. At one point in the late 1800s, an estimated one in three bills in circulation was fake. Ironically, on April 14, 1865—just hours before his assassination—President Abraham Lincoln created the Secret Service to crack down on counterfeiting. (It wasn't until much later that the Secret Service turned most of their attention to the protection of the president, although they still handle counterfeiting.) But even so, forgery remains a rampant crime in the United States and around the world.

HIGH-TECH MONEY

Today, technology has made forgery even tougher to pull off. In money from around the world, you'll see details such as hard-to-reproduce holograms, transparent windows, and watermarks, images that are only visible when you hold the bill up to a light or tilt it. In China, some images on the 100-yuan note change from golden to green or hot pink to green when the angle is adjusted. And in the United States, various banknotes are redesigned every seven to 10 years to tweak anti-counterfeiting technology and forgery-unfriendly security details such as raised printing, watermarks, and color-changing ink.

HOW TO SPOT A FAKE

>> **Not sure if your bill is real? Here are some telltale signs it's legit.**

It's estimated that less than .01 percent of the notes in circulation in the United States are counterfeit.

Shift It
In the United States, denominations of $10 and higher feature color-changing ink in the numeral on the lower right corner of the note. As you tilt the bill, the color should shift from copper to green. Have a $100 bill? Make sure the bell next to Benjamin Franklin changes colors, and you will see a blue 3D security strip featuring tiny images of bells and 100s if you tilt the bill.

See the Light
If you hold any U.S. note $5 and higher up to a light, you should see a watermark and an embedded thread from *both* sides of the bill. The watermark matches the portrait seen on the front of the bill.

Rough Touch
If you move your fingers across the bill, it should feel a bit rough to the touch—a result of the unique printing process and special paper used by the BEP. And on the $100 bill, the area around Benjamin Franklin's shoulder on the left side of the note should feel slightly raised.

Revealing Details
On the U.S. $100 bill, look for itty-bitty images of words—also known as microprinting—on Benjamin Franklin's jacket collar, along the golden quill, and in the borders of the bill. Speaking of borders: They should be crisp and clear. A blurry or out-of-focus border is another sign of a fake.

Seeing Red (and Blue)
Look closely at your cash: You should see tiny red and blue fibers woven in and out within the bill's fabric.

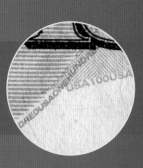

COUNTERFEIT
CRIMINALS BUSTED!

Fake money, real crimes

Modern technology may make it tougher for forgers to produce paper money, but counterfeit rings are still busted around the world nearly every day. Here's a look at how some criminals *almost* cashed in with mega-fake money schemes.

THE PLACE: China
THE DATE: 2017
THE CRIME: Police seized fake notes with a face value of more than 214 million yuan (that's about $33 million in U.S. money), the biggest counterfeiting case in China's modern history. Luckily, none of the counterfeit cash had gone into circulation.

THE PLACE: Peru
THE DATE: 2016
THE CRIME: During a raid known as "Operation Sunset," U.S. and Peruvian agents seized some $30 million in fake American bills from houses and apartment buildings in the capital city of Lima. One of the largest forgery busts in U.S. history, more than 40 people were arrested in the ring—and all of the counterfeit cash was burned.

In 2013, the U.S. $100 bill got a makeover to include a 3D security ribbon and a color-shifting bell.

THE PLACE: London, England
THE DATE: 1999
THE CRIME: Scotland Yard's investigation known as "Operation Mermaid" resulted in the arrest of a gang of forgers who printed fake Scottish notes worth 50 million pounds at the time. The dupes sure looked real since they were printed in various colors, had foil strips to replicate the real money's metallic security strip, and had fake watermarks that were tough to detect by most merchants.

THE PLACE: Uganda
THE DATE: 2019
THE CRIME: An American man living in Uganda was sentenced to six years in jail for making and passing along $1.8 million worth of fake American currency, which he sold online to people living in the United States. To get the bogus cash to his customers, the man packaged it in a pamphlet advertising a nonprofit organization.

THE PLACE: Brazil
THE DATE: 2020
THE CRIME: Cops busted the cybercriminals behind a Brazilian web-based business "Felipe Fakes" which sold—no surprise— fake notes of 50, 100, and 200 reais, the currency of Brazil.

THE FORGER
WHO ALMOST GOT AWAY

▶▶ For an entire decade, Emerich Juettner made a career in counterfeiting. Between 1938 and 1948, Juettner eluded the Secret Service as he continued to create bogus $1 bills from his home, later spending them throughout New York City. Authorities finally nabbed Juettner after his apartment caught fire and firefighters battling the blaze tossed his counterfeiting materials—and a pile of strange-looking $1 bills—on a deserted lot. When some neighborhood kids found the stash of fake cash, they took it to the police, who were later able to connect it back to Juettner.

THE PLACE: Cherry Hill, New Jersey, U.S.A.
THE DATE: 2014
THE CRIME: A ring led by an Israeli man was busted for making counterfeit $50 and $100 bills using a high-tech heat press machine and embossing equipment in a New Jersey warehouse. Over the course of 10 years, the crew is believed to have produced and distributed some $70 million in phony bills.

CHAPTER 4

SPEND IT, SAVE IT, EARN IT!

Sure, you can stash your cash away and save it up until you're ready to buy that one supercool thing you've been eyeing forever. But saving—and spending—money can be a lot more complicated than just filling and emptying a piggy bank. Throughout the world, there are systems in place that allow people to choose to use their money in different ways. Read on for all you need to know about saving, spending—and even earning money off of your own money!

BANK
ON IT

ARE BANKS JUST BUILDINGS FULL OF CASH? NOT QUITE! HERE'S AN OVERVIEW OF HOW THEY OPERATE.

Have you ever been to a bank before? You may have gone with an adult when they needed to deposit a check or stop at an ATM. The act of banking may *seem* pretty simple—you put your money in, you take your money out. But it's not really that straightforward. There's a lot to banks, and they do a lot more than just babysit your money. Here's a look at all the ways banks do business.

THE BEGINNING OF BANKING

The foundation of banking dates back to ancient times. Historians have found evidence of temples and palaces in places like Babylonia, a city-state in ancient Mesopotamia, where farmers would go to borrow seeds. After the harvest, the farmers would pay back the seeds—much like many people do with money today. And for the ancient Greeks, the Temple of Artemis is believed to have been a place where people kept money and debts were collected.

BANKS BOOM

The word "bank" is said to have its roots in the 15th century, when lenders in Italy would conduct transactions from benches, or *bancas* in Italian. The process of depositing and borrowing money from a central location continued to spread throughout Europe. In the United States, Alexander Hamilton, the first secretary of the Treasury under the new Constitution, led the charge to create the Bank of the United States. It opened for business in Philadelphia, Pennsylvania, on December 12, 1791. By 1921, there were more than 30,000 banks in the United States alone.

STASH YOUR CASH

Flash forward to today, and banks look a lot different than they did even a decade ago since so many people opt to bank online. Many transactions, such as sending money to someone else or depositing a payment, are done with a swipe of your finger on an app as opposed to actually going into a bank and physically handing over cash. But the concept of banking remains somewhat the same since those ancient days: Banks still are a secure place to deposit money and make loans.

ACCIDENTAL INVENTION: THE PIGGY BANK!

>> Ever wonder how piggy banks came to be? It was actually an accident! The story goes that throughout Europe during the Middle Ages, people typically stored their money in jars made of an orangey clay known as pygg. Whenever someone had a coin or two to spare, they'd toss them in what became known as a "pygg bank." Hundreds of years later, when English potters were asked to make pygg banks, it's believed that some misinterpreted the request and created them in the shape of pigs. Which, of course, was a hit with customers—especially kids. The concept stuck, and today piggy banks can be found in homes all around the world.

Nearly one in three parents admit to dipping into their kids' piggy bank from time to time.

ALL ACCOUNTED FOR

Banks offer different types of accounts, which are basically arrangements that they'll hold your money, and you can take it out when you need it. The most common types of accounts are savings and checking. A savings account lets you put money aside to use later. A checking account is more for day-to-day expenses and allows you to buy things and pay bills using a debit card, an online or mobile payment, or a paper check.

57

THE BUSINESS OF BANKING

BANKS ARE ALSO BUSINESSES—AND THEY ACTUALLY MAKE MONEY OFF OF YOU. HOW? IT'S ALL ABOUT INTEREST, LOANS, AND FEES.

STEP 1:

You open an account at a bank, depositing $20 of your birthday money and allowance. The bank adds, or credits, the amount of your deposit to your account. You can now access this money whenever you want, and it's guaranteed by the government for most amounts.

STEP 2:

Your money goes into a big pool of money along with money from everyone else who deposits money at that bank.

STEP 3:

The bank makes loans to people who need extra money to pay for expensive items such as houses and cars. Typically, the loan requires people to make a monthly payment, thus paying back the full amount of the loan *plus* interest over time. This interest continues to be charged until the loan is paid off.

STEP 4:

Let's say someone borrows $5,000 and the loan has a 5% annual interest rate, or annual percentage rate (APR). Every month, the borrower pays part of the loan plus interest calculated every month based on the out-standing balance. While the total annual interest charge should be $250 ($5,000 x 5%), the amount will actually be less because payments decrease the loan amount every month.

STEP 5:

The bank profits—or makes money—from collecting interest at a higher rate from its loans than it pays on its deposits, as well as from charging late fees if someone misses a payment on their loan.

STEP 6:

The longer you let your money sit in an interest-paying savings account, the more interest you collect from the bank. The bank adds this interest to your savings account at regular intervals, thereby increasing the amount in your account. Soon, you'll start to earn interest on the interest paid to you. This is known as compounding—and it helps your money grow faster!

ARE YOUR SAVINGS SAFE?

It may seem risky to hand over your money to a bank, which then uses it to pay someone else. But in the United States, the federal government insures up to $250,000 in your account. So even if your bank goes broke (which is unlikely), your savings up to that amount are still totally safe.

MAKE MORE CENTS!

OPEN AN ACCOUNT

Think you're too young for a savings account? Think again! While banks in the United States require you to be 18 to open your own account, you can have a joint or custodial account with an adult at any age. A joint account is shared between you and an adult. You can have access to the money in there, but the adult watches over all of the activity. A custodial account is actually your property, but an adult has control over it until you turn a certain age (usually 18 or 21).

What type of account you choose is up to you and your family. Either way, be sure to look for a bank that's kid-friendly that has low (or no) fees and doesn't require you to have a minimum balance—meaning, it doesn't matter how much or how little money you have in there. And whether you've got $100 saved up or a lot less, having real-life experience with an account of your own will set you up for financial success later on.

EXTRA CREDIT
THE TRUTH ABOUT CREDIT CARDS—AND DEBT

Chances are, you've seen people pay with a credit card just about everywhere you go to shop. In fact, more people prefer to pay with plastic than with actual cash—and that number is only increasing as online shopping becomes more and more the norm. Paying with credit is also a way that people can purchase pricey items, like plane tickets or a new fridge for their kitchen, without having to plunk down big chunks of their savings up front or carry around large amounts of cash. Of course, there's no such thing as free money, and credit card companies are in the business of making money, too. So let's take a swipe at everything there is to know about credit cards!

THE PRICE OF CONVENIENCE

Tapping a credit card seems super easy, but that doesn't mean you're getting something for free! You can use a debit card or a credit card to conveniently access your cash. If you use a *debit* card (which is linked directly to your own checking account), the amount you're charged is instantly taken out of your account. So it's like paying with cash, only it's more convenient since you don't have to carry around cash all the time—and, unlike cash, you can use debit cards online.

With a *credit* card, it's like you're taking out a personal loan with each purchase. Credit card companies (which are typically big banks) keep tabs on every purchase made on the card, and they expect their clients to pay a portion of the money back each month. As with a loan, you can opt to pay the money back in small chunks, or you can try to pay the entire balance at the end of the month. If you choose to pay in portions, you will have to pay interest, which is based on a percentage of your balance and adds to your debt, or the amount of money you owe the bank.

THE DIRT ON DEBT

So how does debt work, exactly? If you borrow $20 from your mom to buy a video game and promise you will pay her back, you are *indebted* to her until she sees that $20 again. Same goes with banks and credit card companies—but, unlike your mom,

they'll keep charging you a fee if you maintain a balance (that is, you don't pay it all off). This is how the credit card companies make their money. According to recent data, each active account makes an average of $180 for credit card companies annually. So if a company has 20,000 active accounts, they'll generate nearly four million dollars in one year!

INTEREST ADDS UP

In the United States, the average credit card debt per household is about $8,000. The cost of having debt can add up, too. Many people wind up paying more in interest than they actually spent on stuff to begin with—and it can take a very long time to pay it all back. Say you pay for groceries with your credit card for $300. Every month, you owe a certain percentage of your balance (the total debt). As long as you have that balance in your account, the credit card company charges you interest on whatever you owe. The interest rate depends on the company and how quickly you pay off your balance. Beware: The interest rates on a credit card tend to be many times higher than the interest rates you earn on savings accounts—meaning, if you need to spend money on something, it's better to use savings than to borrow, and if you absolutely need to use your credit card, you should be mindful of how long you have a balance on it.

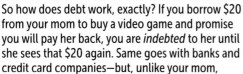

HOW PEOPLE PAY

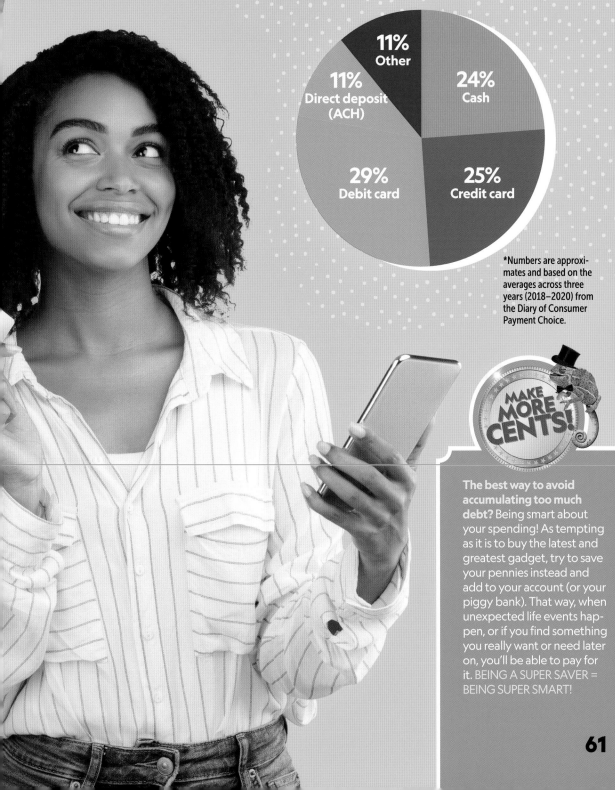

- **11%** Other
- **11%** Direct deposit (ACH)
- **24%** Cash
- **29%** Debit card
- **25%** Credit card

*Numbers are approximates and based on the averages across three years (2018–2020) from the Diary of Consumer Payment Choice.

MAKE MORE CENTS!

The best way to avoid accumulating too much debt? Being smart about your spending! As tempting as it is to buy the latest and greatest gadget, try to save your pennies instead and add to your account (or your piggy bank). That way, when unexpected life events happen, or if you find something you really want or need later on, you'll be able to pay for it. BEING A SUPER SAVER = BEING SUPER SMART!

GROW YOUR MONEY

Ready to start growing your money? Talk to your parent or guardian about the best way you can invest.

Investments can make money out of money.

Now you know about interest—and how you can earn money by letting your savings hang out in a bank account for years and years. That's one way to invest your money. There are other types of investments out there that can yield bigger—and speedier!—results, but there's no such thing as a free lunch! With these investments comes a bit more risk, too.

THE INVESTMENT: GOVERNMENT BONDS

THE WAY IT WORKS: When you buy a U.S. government treasury bond, you are actually lending the U.S. government your money for a fixed period of time (to the maturity date). In exchange, the government promises to pay you interest, typically every six months, based on the face value of the bond. The government repays you the face value of the bond on the maturity date—in short, you get your money back!

POTENTIAL RISK: Generally low. Treasury bonds are backed by the U.S. government, which has never defaulted on a loan.

POTENTIAL REWARD: When the bond finally matures, you will get back the designated value, or face value, of the bond, and you will have received interest along the way.

THE INVESTMENT: MONEY MARKET ACCOUNT

THE WAY IT WORKS: Another type of savings account, money markets usually require a higher minimum balance that you must maintain in your account, so you'll need to keep more than just a few bucks in there, and you are limited on how much you can take out per month.

POTENTIAL RISK: Generally low. Although you can be charged a fee if you can't keep up the minimum balance or if you make too many transactions in one month.

POTENTIAL REWARD: Money market accounts often earn higher interest than traditional savings accounts, which is better for you in the long run.

THE INVESTMENT: CDs

THE WAY IT WORKS: CDs (short for certificates of deposit) are like savings accounts. Only instead of being able to take money out of the account as you please, you agree to let it sit for a fixed period of time.

POTENTIAL RISK: Generally low. If you have to cash out earlier than your agreed-upon terms, you will be dinged with a fee, but otherwise your money is usually well protected in a CD.

POTENTIAL REWARD: More time = more money. CDs allow your money to grow without the temptation of taking it out.

SAFEST

THE INVESTMENT: MUTUAL FUNDS

THE WAY IT WORKS: Each mutual fund represents a group of stocks or bonds. When you buy a mutual fund, you buy a diversified, or varied, group (called a portfolio) of stocks or bonds. This diversification is one of the primary advantages of a mutual fund because it adds some protection from the market's ups and downs compared to owning a single stock.

POTENTIAL RISK: Generally medium. There's always a chance that one of your stocks will drop, but the others may be doing well enough to offset any loss.

POTENTIAL REWARD: By buying a mutual fund, your investment is spread across many more individual stocks or bonds. As a result, you'll earn the average return across all of them and are less likely to be exposed to the losses of any single individual stock.

During World Wars I and II, the U.S. government sold bonds as a way to pay for fighting those wars.

THE INVESTMENT: STOCKS

THE WAY IT WORKS: You buy stock in your favorite company, meaning you now own a tiny piece of it. The hope? The company will grow and make lots of money. You can make money in one of two ways: through dividends (an amount of money from a company's profits paid regularly to that company's shareholders) or through increased value of the stock, called capital gains.

POTENTIAL RISK: Generally medium. Risk varies from stock to stock, and anything from natural disasters to a global pandemic can trigger a company's stock to fall. You also need to review the company's financial statements and related research reports to know whether the stock is continuing to increase in value, or if it might be time to sell.

POTENTIAL REWARD: Owning stocks can earn you dividends, which are ongoing payments from the company while you own its stock, and/or capital gains, which result when you sell the stock above the price you paid for it.

THE INVESTMENT: COLLECTIBLES

THE WAY IT WORKS: Instead of socking your money away, you buy items that you think will increase in value over time. Collectibles may include baseball cards, coins, comic books, toys, and art.

POTENTIAL RISK: Generally very high. There is no guarantee that you will make more money by selling collectibles. The value of certain items may actually go down over time—and there's nothing to protect you from taking a big loss. You also need to keep your collectible somewhere and in good condition, and you'll need to find a buyer who is interested in your particular collectible.

POTENTIAL REWARD: You just may be sitting on something super valuable. If you sell it at the right time (and to the right buyer), you can make some serious money.

RISKIEST

BREAKING DOWN THE STOCK MARKET

STUMPED BY STOCKS? HERE'S MORE ABOUT THE MARKET.

WHAT IS A STOCK?

A stock is a certificate—either in paper or electronic form—that represents a small percentage of ownership of one company. Many major companies are public—that is, their stock can be bought or sold on a stock exchange. Public companies have a certain amount of shares of stock that anyone can buy or sell. So, let's say that Fun Toys Company has a total of 100 shares of stock. If you buy 10 shares, you now own 10 percent of the company.

So, does this mean you can set up an office at the company headquarters and start calling company meetings? Not quite. While you can claim your stake in a tiny fraction of the business, so can other people. Some shareholders do have voting rights and get to participate in corporate decision-making, but that's usually only if you own a large amount of stock. Otherwise, all you have to do is sit back and hope the company is successful, meaning more money for you.

PLAYING THE MARKET

What you do with that stock is up to you. You can choose to keep your stock in Fun Toys for a long time and hope that the value increases as the company's worth grows. Then, if you sell it for a higher value than what you paid for it, you will make a profit!

BLAME IT ON THE WEATHER?

Of course, you can just as easily lose money in the stock market. While the market tends to trend upward, a few factors go into whether it rises or falls. The primary driver of a company's value is its expected earnings. However, everything from a pandemic to natural disasters (such as earthquakes, hurricanes, and even blizzards) to major conflicts (such as a war) to politics (such as an election) can have an impact on the market. Why? Because when scary things happen and life doesn't feel so stable, people are more likely to sell stocks. These trends are tough to predict—and that's what makes the stock market generally riskier than other types of investments.

THE LOWDOWN ON THE DOW AND OTHER STOCK INDEXES

How do we know if the market is rising or falling? There are indexes for that! A stock index is a measurement of the stock market and showcases different groups of companies. Here's a breakdown of the top stock indexes.

THE DOW: Short for the Dow Jones Industrial Average, this index consists of 30 publicly traded companies that represent a big portion of economic activity in the United States.

NASDAQ COMPOSITE: This market index is made up primarily of the biggest publicly traded technology stocks.

S&P 500: This index is a measure of the performance of the top 500 publicly traded companies in the United States, which represent some 80 percent of the total value of the country's stock market.

CRASH!

While a small drop in the stock market is usually nothing to be too concerned about, a crash can cause financial ruin—and disrupt the entire economy of a country. The United States experienced its first major stock market crash in 1929. In the years leading up to it, the economy was experiencing a record high as businesses boomed and people got richer and richer (and bought more and more stocks). As the economy slowed, though, people panicked and began to sell their stocks to collect cash. This triggered a crash that was so severe that many people lost all of their savings and businesses closed for good. The 1929 crash marked the start of the Great Depression, a huge economic downturn that lasted an entire decade.

A RECENT CRISIS

More recently, in September 2008, the stock market tanked by more than 778 points. This led to an economic crisis in the United States—and around the world. Millions of people lost money in the market or their jobs, and many struggled to keep up with their loan payments. This led to the worst recession since 1929.

A PANDEMIC PLUMMET

Then, in March 2020, panic over the COVID-19 pandemic triggered one of the worst stock market crashes in history. Stocks dropped as fears about the virus rose; the dip was so devastating that the New York Stock Exchange stopped trading several times—something that has happened only a few times in its history. As the United States went into lockdown mode, businesses shut down, people lost their jobs, and the economic crash continued. This prompted the U.S. Congress to step in with a $2.3 trillion rescue package as an attempt to boost the economy. It was a scary time for sure, but over the next two years, the stock market and economy recovered to prepandemic levels.

BULL VS. BEAR MARKET

Experts often use these two animals to describe market trends: A "bear" market refers to a decline in stock prices over a few months. A "bull" market means stocks are going up, and money is flowing. While no one is quite sure about the origins of these titles, one common thought is that they're based on the way each animal attacks: Bulls charge by bringing their horns upward, while bears take swipes at their prey with downward paws.

EXCHANGE HERE

A stock exchange is a physical place where people buy and sell stocks. The largest stock exchange in the United States, the New York Stock Exchange, is located on Wall Street in downtown New York City, and there are other important exchanges across the globe, in places like London, Tokyo, and Sydney. At these places, stockbrokers work with clients to monitor the market and buy and sell stocks.

GOING BROKE

WHAT HAPPENS IF YOU RUN OUT OF MONEY?

If you've ever played Monopoly, you know what happens when you run out of money: You go bankrupt and you lose your property—and the game. Going bankrupt in real life isn't all that different, but it's a lot less simple.

A Price to Pay

Companies and individuals are at risk of going bankrupt if they spend or borrow too much and can't pay off their debts. In the United States and other countries around the world, there are bankruptcy laws to protect people drowning in debt. Once you declare bankruptcy (which involves filing paperwork and showing the details of your finances to the government), you are either forgiven your debt or you agree to a repayment plan. Either way, there is a price to pay: You might not be able to get a credit card, take out a loan, or make major purchases again for a long time—not until you can prove that you have enough money coming in to avoid going broke again. And that can make life very hard. But still, it *is* possible to recover ... and even get rich later in life!

FROM RAGS TO RICHES

Famous Figures Who Have Filed for Bankruptcy—and Bounced Back

WALT DISNEY

Early in his career, the "man behind the mouse" had little to his name thanks to the failure of an initial cartoon venture—a company called Laugh-O-gram Films, Inc. As that company dealt with bankruptcy, Walt started the Disney Brothers Cartoon Studio (today known as The Walt Disney Company) with his brother Roy O. Disney in the fall of 1923—and wound up becoming a household name, changing the face of entertainment forever.

P. T. BARNUM

The famous entertainer—he started the Barnum & Bailey Circus in 1871—spent all of his savings building (and rebuilding) his New York City museum, which burned down five times. He eventually took his circus on the road and reaped megabucks, dying in 1891 as a very rich man.

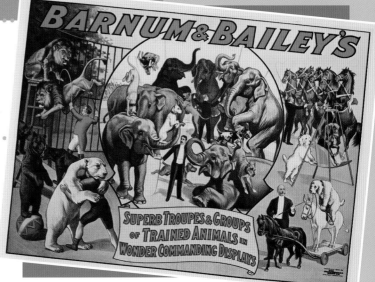

BARNUM & BAILEY'S

SUPERB TROUPES & GROUPS OF TRAINED ANIMALS IN WONDER COMMANDING DISPLAYS

ABRAHAM LINCOLN

From the poorhouse to the White House! When his general store went out of business, Lincoln was left practically penniless. But he worked hard to pay off his debts and eventually became the 16th president of the United States in 1861.

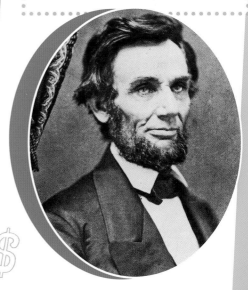

LADY GAGA

When the singer and actress plunked millions into one of her tours, she was left with very little in her bank account. Later, a tour promoter cut her a giant paycheck (to the tune of $40 million) to go back on the road, which helped her rebound. Gaga is said to be worth $150 million today.

CHAPTER 5

MONEY AROUND THE WORLD

There are 195 countries around the world—with each of them operating under different sets of laws, types of governments, and customs. But there's one thing that every place on the planet has in common: Money! While forms of currency vary from country to country, the basic foundations of spending it, saving it, and making it are somewhat the same across the board. Read on to find out how money makes the world go 'round!

RICH LANDS

HOW DO COUNTRIES MAKE MONEY?

All countries are not created the same. Some are huge (like Russia) and some are tiny (like Vatican City). The same goes for their economies. There are some really wealthy places, and others that are not wealthy, and, as a result of a number of factors, are more in the process of developing. These factors might include anything from the climate to histories of colonization. How a country gets rich also comes from a pretty complex formula. But one of the main contributors to wealth is a country's natural resources—and what a country is able to sell, or export, to other countries.

RICH IN RESOURCES

Picture this: You and your friends decide to set up a lemonade stand, and you just so happen to have a lemon tree in your backyard. In order to start up your stand, all you really have to do is pick some lemons, squeeze them, add water and sugar, and you're in business.

But say you don't have easy access to lemons. Instead, you have to go to the grocery store and buy a couple dozen to get going. Before you even start to squeeze, you've already spent money, which you will have to make back by selling extra cups of lemonade.

EXPORTS = INCOME

Here is one of the ways that some countries can get ahead of others. If a country has valuable resources at the ready—such as oil, coal, and precious metals—then it can export them to other countries. It makes money by selling these exports, since other countries need them for important things, such as creating energy. Other countries have to spend money to buy, or import, these resources they don't have, much like how people without access to lemon trees would have to buy lemons before making lemonade.

SHIPSHAPE

Of course, having natural resources isn't the only way a country gets an economic boost. Its location is important, too. Easy access to coastlines is key, as that allows for ports to ship out and receive resources. Landlocked countries—those that are bordered by other countries and have no access to major waterways—are often among the less wealthy nations.

TRADING UP

Other helpful factors? One is having a strong, stable government that regulates the use of one type of currency (like the United States has) as well as the export of natural resources to keep things running smoothly. And when countries have friendly relationships with other countries—especially those that border them—it helps make trading resources a standard and organized process.

ECONOMIC FORECAST: HAZY, HOT—AND BAD FOR FARMING

What does the weather have to do with a country's economy? A country's climate can negatively impact one important aspect of the country's wealth: agriculture. That's because when it's excessively dry, hot, or wet, it is tougher to grow crops that could potentially be sold for a profit. While there are other reasons why developing countries have unstable economies, weather does play a part.

RECIPE FOR RICHES

☑ **Institutions**
The country has a stable, corruption-free government and systems that create, enforce, and apply laws.

☑ **Geography**
The country is located near a major waterway or in a temperate climate.

☑ **Resources**
The country has plenty of valuable resources that it exports to other nations.

☑ **Industries**
A country gets bonus points for having strong industries in pharmaceuticals, biotechnology, and aerospace.

lemonade
25¢

The **WORLD'S** *RICHEST* COUNTRIES

When it comes to wealth, how do certain countries compare?

How do you measure a nation's wealth? It's all about gross domestic product, or GDP. This is a measure of a country's total economy based on the goods and services produced. Because some countries are packed with people (hello, China!) and some are less dense (the Vatican City has fewer than a thousand residents), experts often rank the world's wealthiest nations by GDP per capita, which takes a country's GDP and divides it by its total population. A country's GDP is revisited annually (the figures to the right are from 2019), so the rankings may shift slightly from year to year. But the same group of countries regularly appear at the top of the list.

THE COUNTRY: Norway
POPULATION: 5,372,000
GDP PER CAPITA: About $91,400
WHY IT'S RICH: Norway is a petroleum powerhouse. In fact, oil—found offshore in the seas surrounding the country—makes up about half of its exports.

THE COUNTRY: Singapore
POPULATION: 5,996,000
GDP PER CAPITA: About $61,000
WHY IT'S RICH: A major shipping point, Singapore serves as a connection between mainland Asia and the rest of the world. It's home to many major businesses and is one of the world's largest sellers of microchips for computers and smartphones.

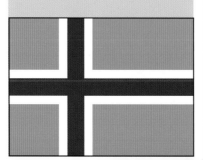

72

A NEW TECH INNOVATION HUB

NAIROBI, KENYA

» Challenged by hot weather, droughts, food shortages, and conflict, some countries in Africa face serious economic problems. But there are also countries that are seeing more and more dollar signs lately, thanks to an abundance of agriculture, natural resources, and trade. Among them? Kenya, aka "Silicon Savannah," which has made advances in technology and serves as the headquarters for many mobile-based businesses. This has brought on more jobs and boosted the economy. And Kenya's not the only country in Africa seeing a boom in technological innovation: From 2015 to 2020, African tech start-ups grew 46 percent in comparison to only 8 percent growth globally.

THE COUNTRY: Qatar
POPULATION: 2,364,000
GDP PER CAPITA: About $60,000
WHY IT'S RICH: Qatar is home to some 13 percent of the global supply of oil, a natural resource that rakes in tens of billions of dollars for the country each year.

THE COUNTRY: United States
POPULATION: About 321,004,000
GDP PER CAPITA: About $54,000
WHY IT'S RICH: Aside from a strong government, plenty of natural resources, and a booming tech industry, many of the world's cars are produced in the United States, contributing to its wealth.

THE COUNTRY: Germany
POPULATION: About 80,458,000
GDP PER CAPITA: About $48,100
WHY IT'S RICH: Germany exports a variety of goods, with automobiles—including brands such as BMW, Mercedes-Benz, Audi, and Volkswagen—topping the list.

THE EXCHANGE RATE
EXPLAINED
HOW TO FIGURE OUT WHAT COSTS WHAT IN A DIFFERENT COUNTRY

Fast forward a few years: You're all grown up and headed to Morocco (as a National Geographic Explorer on the hunt for dinosaur bones, of course!). You can't wait to get there and start your adventure into the Sahara. But wait—you take a look at the train fares, and the prices are a lot different from what you're used to. How will you figure out how much the train trip costs?

ENTER THE EXCHANGE RATE

In a nutshell, the exchange rate reflects how one country's currency compares to another nation's. To figure out what you're really paying for a product in another country, you'll have to flex the ol' math muscles. Here's how it works:

Say you want to buy a hat to keep you protected in the hot Moroccan sun. The price tag says 179 dirham (the name of Moroccan currency). At the moment, the dirham to dollar exchange rate is .11. So, if you are changing dirham to dollar, you'd need to multiply .11 (the exchange rate) x 179 (the cost in dirham). Meaning that hat is going to cost you almost $20.00 (U.S.).

IT'S TRICKY

Making things even trickier? The exchange rate is always changing. Sometimes several times a day! The number is based on several factors, including the state of a country's economy. And, of course, what you pay varies from place to place. If you're traveling to Kenya, for example, you might expect an exchange rate of .01 (or 100 shillings to 1 dollar)! So if you buy a soda there you may expect to cough up 200 shillings—the equivalent of just two bucks in the States.

CASHING IN

So how do you change up your money? Banks, money-changer booths (located in most airports and train stations), and ATMs will convert your cash into foreign currency. (But take note: There's usually a fee that comes along with the changeover.) And if your parents ever do allow you to use a credit or debit card, you need to be extra careful about how much you're spending as you swipe.

THE POWER OF THE DOLLAR

>> If you've had the opportunity to travel to other countries, you might notice that the U.S. dollar is accepted in many places around the world. So what makes the dollar so universal? It has a lot to do with the United States' stable government and powerful economy. And the value of the dollar stays mostly the same, unlike the currencies in some other countries that tend to fluctuate more frequently.

Currency on Every Continent

From Africa to Antarctica, how money varies in different parts of the planet

Early American colonists adopted the dollar sign from Spanish-Mexican currency—which is why the symbol for both the peso and the dollar is $.

NORTH AMERICA

The U.S. dollar rules throughout North America, but there are actually dozens more currencies used on the continent, including the Eastern Caribbean dollar, the Canadian dollar, and the Mexican peso.

Canada
NORTH AMERICA
United States

PACIFIC OCEAN

ATLANTIC OCEAN

Mexico

OCEANIA
French Polynesia (France)

Ecuador
Peru
Brazil
SOUTH AMERICA

Chile

SOUTH AMERICA

Of the 15 distinct areas that make up South America—12 countries, two British territories, and one French territory—all but Ecuador, which uses the U.S. dollar, have their own currency. Among the strongest South American currencies? Peru's sol, which reflects the country's quickly growing economy.

Every Brazilian real (pronounced hey-al) features an animal native to the country—like a tamarin and jaguar—on the back of the banknote.

Antarctica is the only place on the planet where the land isn't officially owned by anyone.

MAKE MORE CENTS!

Has your great aunt traveled around the world? Ask her if she has any cool currency she can share with you. Not only can you admire the different designs, but you can practice your math by figuring out how much each coin or bill is worth in U.S. dollars.

ANTARCTICA

There is no Antarctic currency—or any actual banks on the continent, for that matter. There are two ATMs at U.S. research stations that dispense U.S. dollars, which scientists use to pay for everything from meals to haircuts at research centers.

EUROPE

You'll find several currencies used throughout Europe, but the euro is by far the most common. However, places like Denmark (Danish krone), the U.K. (British pound), Iceland (Icelandic krona), Russia (ruble), and Switzerland (Swiss franc) do stick to their own make of money.

The British pound, dating back to the eighth century, is the world's oldest currency that's still in use.

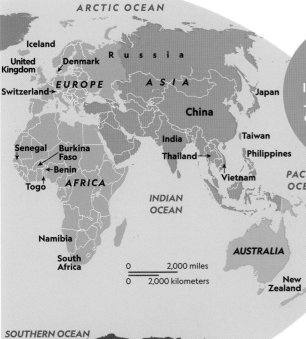

ARCTIC OCEAN

Iceland
United Kingdom
Denmark
R u s s i a
EUROPE
A S I A
Switzerland
Japan
China
India
Taiwan
Senegal
Burkina Faso
Benin
Thailand
Philippines
Togo
AFRICA
Vietnam
PACIFIC OCEAN
INDIAN OCEAN
Tuvalu
OCEANIA
Namibia
AUSTRALIA
Fiji
South Africa

0 — 2,000 miles
0 — 2,000 kilometers

New Zealand

SOUTHERN OCEAN
McMurdo Station (ATMs located here)
A N T A R C T I C A

With features like watermarks, holograms, and luminescent ink, the Japanese yen is one of the most difficult currencies to counterfeit.

ASIA

Each of Asia's 49 countries uses its own money. But the Chinese yuan and the Indian rupee are typically accepted throughout Asia.

AUSTRALIA, NEW ZEALAND, AND OCEANIA

Down under, the dollar rules, whether it's the Australian dollar, the New Zealand dollar, or the U.S. dollar. Meanwhile, many of the small countries and dependent territories that make up the rest of Oceania have their own currency, such as the Fijian dollar or the CFP franc, used in French Polynesia.

The Australian dollar is also called a buck, dough, or the Aussie.

AFRICA

There are 54 African countries, and just a few of them have a common currency. The most universal? The West African CFA franc is used in 15 countries, including Benin, Burkina Faso, Senegal, and Togo. But some countries have more than one official currency. In Namibia, for example, you can use the Namibian dollar as well as the South African rand.

South African bills featuring the face of famed former president Nelson Mandela are known as "Randelas."

INSTANT
MILLIONS

What could you do with $100? Thanks to the lopsided values of goods and services from country to country,* you could be a "millionaire" (or close to it) in these spots around the world. But how far will your millions stretch? Find out!

THE PLACE: Vietnam
For $100 (U.S.), you'd get ... about 2.3 million Vietnamese dong.
You can pick one of the following:
... 46 meals at a restaurant
... 26 movie tickets
... 1 pair of sneakers
... 18 gallons (68 L) of milk
... 9 months of internet access

THE PLACE: Indonesia
For $100 (U.S.), you'd get ... about 1.4 million Indonesian rupiah.
You can pick one of the following:
... 28 lunches out at a restaurant
... 28 movie tickets
... 1.5 pairs of sneakers
... 20 gallons (76 L) of milk
... 3 months of internet access

TICKET
ADMIT ONE
DATE 27.07.2018 · 21:00

THE PLACE: Guinea

For $100 (U.S.), you'd get … about 900,000 Guinean francs.

You can pick one of the following:

… 28 gallons (106 L) of gas
… 60 tubes of toothpaste
… 16 gallons (60 L) of milk
… 2 months of internet access
… 360 rolls of toilet paper

THE PLACE: Uzbekistan

For $100 (U.S.), you'd get … about one million Uzbek so'm.

You can pick one of the following:

… 39 combo meals at a fast-food restaurant
… 70 dozen eggs
… 11 months of internet access
… 2 pairs of sneakers
… 130 tubes of toothpaste

THE PLACE: Laos

For $100 (U.S.), you'd get … about 1.1 million Laotian kip.

You can pick one of the following:

… 21 combo meals at a fast-food restaurant
… 55 pounds (25 kg) of apples
… 4 months of internet access
… 93 hours of housecleaning services
… 36 haircuts

*Since exchange rates change, these numbers are just estimates!

THE CULTURE
OF MONEY

UNIQUE TRADITIONS, CUSTOMS, AND PRACTICES FROM AROUND THE WORLD

SMART SAVERS

Some people in Panama make sure they've got enough saved for big celebrations like Christmas by making monthly installments into a *caja de ahorros* (a special savings account) throughout the year. Each December, they cash out the full amount to spend on gifts.

ALL IN THE WRIST!

In Laos, there's a tradition of blessing a major life event—such as a wedding or a new baby—by rolling up bills in a banana leaf and tying it to the guest of honor's wrist with a white cotton string. The belief? That if you keep the string tied for at least three days, a special blessing will come true.

THE ENVELOPE PLEASE

In China, it's customary for parents and grandparents to hand out small red envelopes full of cash to kids to mark the Lunar New Year. Known as lucky money, the gift is meant to symbolize a year of good fortune for the younger generation.

DOLLAR DANCE

At many Greek, Polish, and Ukrainian weddings, it's a tradition for the bride and groom to dance around the reception while guests take turns pinning cash on their clothes. It's a simple and festive way to start the new couple off with some extra spending money.

RICH $UPERSTITIONS!

In some areas of ...

RUSSIA ... never whistle at home. It may cause you financial loss!

MEXICO ... wear yellow underwear if you want cash to come your way.

FRANCE ... never place bread upside down on the table, to avoid going poor—and hungry!

LITHUANIA ... a bird pooping on your head may mean you're about to get rich.

CHINA ... eat oysters, egg rolls, peanuts, pineapple, and rice to get rich during Lunar New Year.

ITALY ... spot a spider at night and you might get rich quick!

THE PHILIPPINES ... crack an egg with two yolks and you might expect double the money soon.

TURKEY ... hold gold in your hand in a dream as you sleep and you'll attract more money in real life.

UNITED STATES ... find a penny, pick it up ... all day long, you'll have good luck!

COMMUNITY CREDIT

In Kenya, when someone wants to open up a business or start a project that's aimed to help the community, sometimes the local people step in instead. Through a custom known as harambee (Swahili for "all pull together"), members of a community pitch in to help pay for the project. Now those are some nice neighbors!

CASH ONLY

In Germany, there's a saying: *geld stinkt nicht,* which translates to "cash doesn't stink." What's that mean? That many Germans turn their noses up at credit cards—and favor cash so they're more aware of their spending (and, as a result, have less debt).

THE GLOBAL EFFORT

A LOOK AT THE IMF AND THE WORLD BANK

With so many different countries—and currencies—around the world, it's a tough task to keep it all in check. But there are two major groups that attempt to do just that. The International Monetary Fund (better known as the IMF) and the World Bank are separate branches of the United Nations, an organization of countries focused on keeping peace around the planet. Together, the IMF and the World Bank help countries develop their economies. But there are definite differences between the two.

THE IMF

The United States has contributed about $154 billion to the IMF.

ESTABLISHED: 1944
LOCATION: Headquarters in Washington, D.C., with offices around the world
ITS MISSION: The IMF originally began as a way to help countries struggling financially after World War II. Today, the IMF is made up of representatives of some 190 countries, with the purpose of overseeing the stability of the world's monetary system. Part of this includes keeping exchange rates stable, bailing out countries in money trouble, and smoothing out financial relationships among different nations.
THE IMF IN ACTION: With a total of one trillion dollars to lend to member countries, the IMF acts as a life raft to countries struggling with debt. When Pakistan's economy tanked after a 2005 earthquake, the country received a large loan from the IMF. Later, in 2019, Pakistan accepted another six billion dollars from the IMF, which the country is expected to pay back eventually. And when Greece struggled to keep its economy from collapsing, the IMF stepped in with one of its largest loans ever, at about $145 billion. The IMF also responded to countries that needed emergency financial assistance because of the COVID-19 pandemic, beginning in 2020.

THE WORLD BANK

ESTABLISHED: 1944
LOCATION: Washington, D.C., with offices worldwide
ITS MISSION: The World Bank focuses on offering financial assistance and other services to countries with developing economies. It also invests in projects that can bring a boost to local communities, such as renewable energy and agriculture. This is all in an effort to reduce poverty, or the state of being extremely poor (defined by the World Bank as those who live on less than $1.90 a day) around the world.
THE WORLD BANK IN ACTION: With the help of the World Bank, Sri Lanka recently rose from a developing country that was recovering from nearly 30 years of civil war to a lower-middle-income nation. Currently, the World Bank is putting extra effort into initiatives focusing on solar power and sustainable energy. The Bank's hope? To curb climate change, especially in developing nations, where rising temperatures can hurt their economies.

In 2020, the World Bank provided two billion dollars to help buy and distribute COVID-19 vaccines for developing countries.

NOT-SO-BASIC BANKS

Wow-worthy and wacky spots to get money around the world!

GLOW UP

WHERE: Hong Kong, China

This soaring skyscraper—the first building outside the United States to break the 1,000-foot (305-m) mark—is home to the Bank of China. Stretching 1,204 feet (367 m) tall, it's one of the world's tallest corporate headquarters. And it's one of the prettiest, too: At night, the building's shiny, diamond-shaped surface lights up, making it look like a giant glittering crystal.

SKY HIGH

WHERE: Hunza Valley, Pakistan

Need some cash as you're crossing the Khunjerab Pass? Simply stop by the machine near the border of Pakistan and China. At 15,397 feet (4,693 m) above sea level, it's the world's highest ATM!

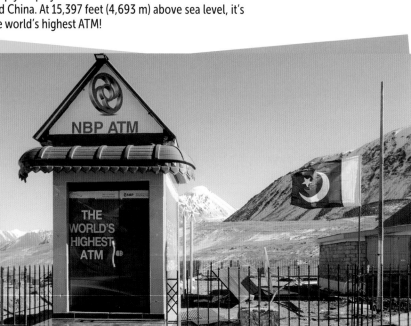

WORK OF ART

WHERE: Berlin, Germany

Famed architect Frank Gehry designed the DZ Bank building, featuring the giant four-story sculpture known as "Horse's Head," which serves as a conference room. Topping it off? A glass ceiling crisscrossed with stainless steel to give it the look of a spider's web.

BLAST FROM THE PAST

WHERE: New York City

Back in the late 1800s, a place on the southern tip of Manhattan in New York City was home to a steamship company that managed luxe ocean liners. Today the building serves a bank, but you can still spot subtle hints from its past: Customers can opt to enter through one of two entrances, one marked "First Class" and the other "Cabin Class."

FLOAT ON

WHERE: Indonesia

Villagers in some of the most far-flung archipelagos of Indonesia cash checks and make withdrawals from a floating bank branch. The bank is housed on a boat named *Teras BRI Kapal* and is equipped with some 11 tellers and an ATM, with the aim of making banking accessible to all.

ONCE A BANK ...

>> ... and now a McDonald's? In Kristiansand, Norway, hungry visitors can pick up a value meal in a marble-columned building that used to house a bank. The downtown location doesn't use the bank's original door (customers enter through the side), but otherwise it has kept its classical look.

85

CHAPTER 6

THE FUTURE OF MONEY

As more and more people turn to technology to assist them in their day-to-day tasks, the world of finance has had to quickly evolve to meet these demands. Now it's possible for people to deposit checks, send someone money, and even pay for products from a phone or computer. And this is just the beginning: Many more shifts are in store having to do with how we spend and earn money. Here's a look at the ever changing technology of finance—and what money may look like in the not-too-distant future.

SMARTER CARDS

A timeline of credit card technology

Paying with a credit card can be as quick and easy as it comes (as long as people remember to pay their bill each month!). The card is swiped or inserted into a reader and voilà—thanks to a tiny computer chip inside, the deal is done. But these pieces of plastic weren't always so sophisticated. Here's a look at how credit cards have evolved throughout the years.

1888

Author Edward Bellamy is the first person known to use the term "credit card," which he writes about in his book *Looking Backward*. Bellamy's fictitious card—which represented a share of the national wealth, which every citizen received—plants the seed for what is to come for credit cards.

1928

Little metal plates known as Charga-Plates start popping up in department stores. When customers buy an item, the cashier uses special paper and a tiny press to take an imprint of the raised lettering and numbers on the card. (This method of imprinting will stick around until the 1970s.) The Charga-Plate not only helps stores keep track of transactions, but it allows customers to keep a tab at certain stores—which they can pay off periodically.

1946

A banker named John Biggins develops the Charg-It card, issued by the Flatbush National Bank of Brooklyn in New York City. Customers can use the card at nearby stores, with the bank later settling payments for them.

1950

Businessman Frank McNamara comes up with the idea for a cardboard charge card after he forgot his wallet while dining out at a New York City restaurant. Thinking there should be an alternative for paying other than cash, he creates the Diners Club, used mostly to pay for meals and entertainment, with members paying off their charges at the end of each month. The card is made of cardboard until the 1960s, when it goes plastic.

1958

Bank of America releases the BankAmericard to customers in California, U.S.A., as the first general-purpose credit card. (American Express also introduces a charge card in the United States and Canada in the same year.) The idea spreads to other banks around the country. By 1976, the card becomes known as the Visa card.

e-Shopping

1971

Credit cards all over the world get a makeover with a magnetic stripe. First developed by tech company IBM for train tickets in London and San Francisco, California, the "mag stripe" contains info about the cardholder and card. This allows the person's identifying info to be logged and transmitted swiftly and more securely with a swipe.

When he was first developing the mag stripe, engineer Forrest Parry used a household iron to secure the strip onto a plastic card.

1986

Reward cards make their debut, linking credit purchases to a points system. Banks and companies encourage cardholders to use their cards more by offering points for money spent. The points can be traded in for cash, plane tickets, and other discounts.

1994

Internet-based companies such as Amazon (1994), eBay (1995), and PayPal (1998) launch, and electronic payments done online—also known as e-commerce—reach record highs.

2004

Mini credit cards make their way into the mainstream. These tiny cards—nearly half the size of today's standard credit card—are made to conveniently hang from a key chain and reduce wallet clutter. But they don't quite catch on and are mostly phased out within a few years.

2015

The EMV (short for Europay, MasterCard, and Visa) computer chip is first introduced in Europe as a more secure alternative to the mag stripe. Later adopted in the United States and by most major credit card companies, the chip technology makes the data on the card much harder to hack than the mag stripe does. Experts say the EMV chip reduces credit card fraud by 76 percent.

2016 and beyond

Contactless payments—or cards that contain a special technology that will allow you to tap or wave the card above a reader—become more mainstream. This method continues to provide a much faster and more secure transaction than standard credit cards.

CURIOUS COLLECTION

Some people collect coins. And some people collect ... credit cards? At least that's the case with Zheng Xiangchen, a man from China who has a collection of some 1,562 valid credit cards to his name—a world record. To compare, the average American has about three cards in their name, according to a recent study. At least that way you can fit them all in one wallet!

89

PRICE
CHECK!

A look at the cost of popular items in the past, present, and future

In the United States, can you imagine paying just two dollars for a brand-new pair of pajamas? Or how about forking over more than $100,000 for a car? As times change, so does the cost of everyday items. Why? Over time, prices change as an economy grows and people earn more ... but the money earned is worth less than it was in the past. (See "Inflation, explained" sidebar for more info!) Here's a look at average prices of popular things 50 years ago, prices in the present, and a projection of what they may cost 50 years in the future.

The "future" price reflects an average inflation rate of 2.5 percent of the U.S. dollar.

A NEW BIKE
PAST: $40.95
PRESENT: $179
FUTURE: $600

A NEW CAR
PAST: $3,000
PRESENT: $47,000
FUTURE: $153,760

WALKIE-TALKIES
PAST: $8.99
PRESENT: $30
FUTURE: $98

FLANNEL PJ'S
PAST: $1.99
PRESENT: $30
FUTURE: $98

CHEAPER TECH
Thanks to technology becoming more and more available to the masses, the price of many gadgets and electronics such as digital cameras, computers, and TVs is actually going down—and they may continue to be more and more affordable as the years go on.

BOTTLE OF MOUTH-WASH (20 OZ /591 ML)
PAST: $1
PRESENT: $4
FUTURE: $13

1 POUND (.45 KG) OF STRAWBERRIES
PAST: $0.49
PRESENT: $3.29
FUTURE: $10.76

BOARD GAME
PAST: $4.29
PRESENT: $15
FUTURE: $50

A BOX OF CEREAL
PAST: $0.49
PRESENT: $3.79
FUTURE: $12.40

INFLATION, EXPLAINED

Why do prices keep changing? It's all about inflation. Generally speaking, inflation is when a given currency has less purchasing power over time. That means that the value of the currency is going down and the cost of common goods and services is going up. This chain reaction drives up the cost of many everyday items, such as food, gas, and even the price of homes. This means you can get less for your money than you used to be able to get. So while it may seem like your parents paid a lot less for things when they were kids than you do now (50 cents for a soda? Unheard of!), things weren't really *that* much cheaper back in the day. The dollar just stretched a lot further, so even though people made less money, things also cost less.

BITCOINS AND BEYOND

THE DISH ON DIGITAL MONEY

Y ou may have heard friends or family members mention cryptocurrency. Or maybe you watch the news and have heard of it there. Why is everyone talking about it? Read on to find out what it is and how it works.

BIT BY BIT

Before there was email, there was snail mail. And before there was cryptocurrency, there was conventional currency—money that is backed by a government (aka fiat currency). For decades, fiat currency has been the accepted form of payments and exchanges of money within a country.

VIRTUAL CURRENCY

Enter cryptocurrency. Around 2009, something called Bitcoin came onto the scene, which exists only in a virtual world. So, instead of having actual coins and bills you can see and feel and watch pile up in a piggy bank, you have a stash of digital dollars tucked away on the internet. Today, Bitcoin is the most recognizable form of cryptocurrency, but there are more than a thousand other kinds out there.

In September 2018, the word "bitcoin" was added to the *Official Scrabble Players Dictionary*.

MONEY MYSTERY

The story goes that Bitcoin was invented by a Japanese man named Satoshi Nakamoto. The thing is, no one knows who Nakamoto actually is. After introducing Bitcoin to the world by writing a nine-page paper describing a plan for this new form of currency, Nakamoto remained anonymous. While several people have come forward falsely claiming to be him (and one man even filed a lawsuit to prove that *he* is Bitcoin's creator), Nakamoto's identity may always remain a mystery.

HOW CRYPTOCURRENCY WORKS

So how does it work? To start, all transactions happen online. And they are not regulated by the government, like traditional currency is. People exchange cryptocurrency among each other without going through a bank. If you pay for something with cryptocurrency, your wallet ID (a series of numbers and letters unique to each user) appears in a public log, known as a blockchain. Each digital coin has its own blockchain, and they're different from one another.

VARIED VALUE

The biggest difference between cryptocurrency and regular money? Its value! Cryptocurrency has no fixed worth. Its cost goes up and down, like gas prices. Recently, the price of one bitcoin has gone from around $29,000 to $41,000 and back down again. (But you can buy pieces of one bitcoin, known as satoshis, for a lot less.) So what's up with the crazy fluctuation of the cost of cryptocurrency? It's all about supply and demand. The more people want cryptocurrency, the more it'll cost. And again, unlike regular currency, its value is not regulated or controlled by a government.

CREATING CRYPTOCURRENCY

So how is cryptocurrency created and what is it? All cryptocurrency is "mined." Unlike gold miners who used pickaxes and elbow grease to pluck shiny nuggets from the soil, cryptocurrency miners on computers compete to solve complicated math calculations and puzzles. Once a problem is solved, a new "block" is added to the chain and more cryptocurrency is created. The miner is then rewarded with cryptocoins, which they can then keep or sell.

BUY AND STORE

To get cryptocurrency, people go online and buy it from websites called exchanges. From there, it's stored in a digital wallet, which is a password-protected space on a phone, in the cloud, on a computer, or on a flash drive.

THE DARK SIDE OF CRYPTOCURRENCY

Cryptocurrency only exists online, so it's an easy target for hackers looking to make quick money. In fact, reports of cryptocurrency crimes—which include everything from straight-up stealing to scams—have increased 312 percent a year on average since 2016. If crypto isn't stored in a supersecure place online, hackers can gain access to crypto wallets or breach entire cryptocurrency exchanges and collect millions. Even scarier? Because cryptocurrency can be exchanged anonymously and privately, it can be used as a way to fund terrorist organizations or other criminal activities, posing a serious security risk. As a result, governments around the world are working hard to target and stop crypto criminals.

THE FUTURE OF CRYPTOCURRENCY

Because cryptocurrency isn't something you can hold in your hand (or put into an actual wallet) and because it's not regulated by a government, it has its share of skeptics, including some leading economists and financial experts. So while the jury is still out on whether cryptocurrency will be the wave of the future, currently all cryptocurrencies combined account for less than about 0.7 percent of all the world's money.

IS BITCOIN BAD FOR THE ENVIRONMENT?

In a word, yes. Worldwide, Bitcoin mining operations use more energy than the entire nation of Sweden, according to the Cambridge Bitcoin Electricity Consumption Index. And a single Bitcoin transaction uses the same amount of power as the average American household consumes in a month. While these stats are staggering, efforts are underway to reduce the consumption and carbon emissions from crypto mining, an important move in curbing climate change.

In 2010, someone used 10,000 bitcoin to purchase two pizzas.

CASHING OUT

THE WAY WE PAY IS CHANGING. HERE'S HOW.

NO-CASH COUNTRIES

Certain nations—including Sweden, China, Denmark, and the U.K.—are well on their way to becoming totally cashless. The motive? Not only is it easier for businesses and individuals to keep track of their money (as every transaction is digitally recorded), but a cashless system eliminates the issue of counterfeit currency. And some store owners believe the removal of cash lowers the risk of robberies. Of course, hackers could continue to be a big problem in the future for many cashless methods.

THE FUTURE IS NOW: In Sweden, about 80 percent of people use a card to pay for purchases. Digital payments via card or apps are so widely accepted that many Swedes no longer carry cash. It's even common to see kids paying for items with their own debit cards!

SMARTER PHONES

Forget change purses and wallets. In the future, your phone might be the keeper of your money. By storing your info from a credit card or debit card in a mobile wallet on your phone, you can buy things quickly and relatively safely, since your phone is password protected and can be shut down remotely if stolen. No need for cash, which can be lost or stolen.

THE FUTURE IS NOW: More and more people around the world are using mobile wallets. In fact, it's estimated that by 2023 there will be 1.31 billion mobile payment transaction users worldwide, up from 950 million users in 2019.

WITH THE BAND

Another form of contactless payment, smart wearables let you pay with the flick of the wrist. How? Funds are loaded on a watch or a wristband containing a computer chip that's linked to a credit or debit card. When making a purchase, just wave your wearable near a sensor and money will be deducted from your digital wallet or charged to your account.

THE FUTURE IS NOW: You can see this technology in action at Walt Disney World in Florida, U.S.A., where MagicBands allow visitors to make purchases throughout the park without ever having to reach for their wallets.

NFC
HOW WEARABLES WORK

>> Most contactless payment systems rely on a complex technology called near-field communication (NFC). It works by picking up info when you're within a small distance of a scanner to wirelessly transfer data. So when a person goes to pay, they just wave their wearable (or phone) and off they go.

SPEAK UP

Hello!

Craving a slice of deep-dish pepperoni? Simply shout "Order me a pizza" into your smart speaker and your pie will soon be on its way. Too good to be true? Nope! This kind of voice-based purchasing will be happening more and more in homes. Digital speakers will be able to take your request to buy something, order it, and use a digital payment to make the transaction.

THE FUTURE IS NOW: The Alexa smart speaker is currently equipped to process simple orders on Amazon via a voice request.

LEAVE THE LINES BEHIND

Instead of making people wait in line, some stores are moving toward cashier-less, checkout-free shopping experiences. A shopper downloads a specific app to enter the store and take what they want. Using a combo of overhead cameras, weight sensors, and supersmart technology, the store keeps track of the items the shopper collects and automatically charges their account.

THE FUTURE IS NOW: Amazon is already using "Just Walk Out" technology at stores in locations including Washington, D.C., and Bellevue, Washington, U.S.A. Walmart and 7-Eleven are also testing out cashier-less stores.

KEEPING CASH AROUND

>> Many businesses may be jumping on the cashless bandwagon, but not everyone is in favor of going all digital. In fact, lawmakers in U.S. states including New York, Pennsylvania, Massachusetts, and California have passed bills banning cashless businesses, stating that they discriminate against minors as well as those who may not have bank accounts or credit cards. The punishment for businesses that are caught cashless in New York? A fine of up to $1,000.

95

COOL INVENTION$

Gizmos and gadgets you may one day use at the checkout counter and beyond

MODERN MONEY MACHINE
THE INVENTION: Cryptocurrency ATM
WHY IT'S COOL: A few areas now offer cryptocurrency ATMs. People scan their hand from the screen and then move funds to or from their virtual accounts. And if they need actual cash, some machines let customers transfer their bitcoins into actual bucks.

BANK BOT
THE INVENTION: Robot bank
WHY IT'S COOL: This bot takes your savings to the next level. Acting like a mini ATM, it allows you to slip your cash through the slot and then punch in a code when you want to make a withdrawal. But that's not all this bot does—it also speaks and doubles as a night-light. Brilliant!

CHARGED UP
THE INVENTION: Phone-charging wallet
WHY IT'S COOL: This wallet brings new meaning to "charge" card! It may look like a basic billfold, but the wallet has a tiny sewn-in pocket inside that contains a rechargeable phone battery. Simply plug your phone into the battery for a full charge while you're on the go.

SMARTER SAVINGS

THE INVENTION: Virtual bank for kids

WHY IT'S COOL: Bankaroo, a digital app, lets kids play around with virtual money to learn more about saving, collecting interest, and setting financial goals. Although there's no real money exchanged on the app, you'll still get a good, uh, *cents* of what saving and spending are all about.

SO KEY

THE INVENTION: Contactless payment key chain

WHY IT'S COOL: You don't need your smartphone or wallet nearby when you go to buy something with this key chain. A chip inside it is linked directly to your bank account, so simply wave your keys in front of a scanner to pay and you'll be on your way.

BY THE NECK

THE INVENTION: Wearable cryptocurrency wallet

WHY IT'S COOL: Some people who use cryptocurrency keep it on a flash drive, but with this still-in-development wearable wallet, a person stores their cryptocurrency around their neck! The gadget also uses the unique rhythm of a person's heartbeat to identify them and instantly logs them into a smartphone app so they can access their funds—meaning they don't have to remember one more password.

MAKE MORE CENTS!

Have a million-dollar idea of your own? Write it down! You have the power to create something amazing, so don't let your age stop you. If you're super confident that your new product can really make a difference one day, ask a guardian for help and look into entering an invention contest for kids. If anything, you'll get to really think through your idea and get practice sharing your original thoughts. And even if that idea doesn't turn into the next greatest gadget, if you keep at it, maybe one day one of your ideas will!

A LOOK AHEAD

What will banks look like in, say, 20 years? Take a look inside this spot in Shanghai, China, to see some fun futuristic features that you may see in your local branch one day.

Just need to check your account balance? You don't need to go beyond Little Dragon. She can read your bank card and let you know how much you've got stashed in your savings, among other info.

Enter the bank through an electronic turnstile. Sensors on each gate scan your face and then use facial recognition to pull up your info and allow access inside.

Walk into the bank and be greeted by "Little Dragon," a chatty robot that serves as a branch manager. She meets customers at the electronic gate at the front, chats with them, finds out what they need, and guides them inside.

Once inside, you'll go to an ATM to complete transactions such as opening an account or transferring money. Need help? Another robot is there to answer any questions.

If you have a pressing matter where you need to talk to an actual person, you can head to the virtual reality (VR) room and connect to a bank employee remotely.

It's not just about money within this branch: Customers can also hang out and tap into a library of some 50,000 e-books, grab snacks from a vending machine, or play games in a VR zone.

This bank isn't *totally* human free: Security guards monitor all of the comings and goings of customers from surveillance cameras in a separate room—and will step in if they see anything suspicious going down.

WHY ROBOTS?

>> It's not like robots will be running *all* banks in the future, but this concept follows the trend of the cashless shops, restaurants, and other retailers that are relying more and more on artificial intelligence (AI) to take care of business. Because robots are programmed to do very specific tasks quickly and efficiently, one study predicts that more than 150,000 mobile robots will be used in retail locations around the world by 2025. So get used to seeing a robot where you shop—or bank.

99

OUT OF THIS WORLD

THE SCOOP ON SPACE CURRENCY

Here's an exciting prospect: Humans may one day be able to travel to—and even live on!—Mars. And if that happens, how will people pay for things on another planet?

NO CASH IN SPACE ...

For starters, there won't be any cash, coins, or credit cards in space. Even though by the time people are on Mars, we may be using technology to create artificial gravity in some areas, a general lack of gravity throughout space means items travel at superhigh speeds. Typically harmless paper bills and metal coins might transform into floating weapons that could slice through the protective suit you'd have to wear in space. Besides, it would be too tough to make money as we know it on Mars because of the environment and all of the equipment needed—and hauling stacks of cash in a spaceship would add extra weight, costing more fuel.

... AND NO CREDIT CARDS, EITHER

As for credit cards? The high levels of cosmic radiation in the atmosphere would likely scramble the magnetic strip on cards or cause the computer chip to go haywire, meaning there'd be no swiping in space.

IT'S INTERGALACTIC!

Instead, experts predict the creation of a space currency. Back in 2007, one company came up with a concept called Quasi Universal Intergalactic Denomination, also known as QUID. The idea:

round disks made of a special material that's heat-resistant and contains no chemicals that could hurt space tourists. QUID would be marked with tracking codes in order to prevent counterfeiting, or making and distributing fake forms of the currency. While the idea never, well, blasted off, it shed some light on what space currency may one day look like.

GOING DIGITAL

Some sort of cryptocurrency could possibly be an option, as well. One concept: Marscoin, designed specifically for the red planet. But there's one big problem: At millions of miles away from a Wi-Fi signal, it would be tough to log online to access your digital wallet. So until scientists can develop a way to generate a strong Wi-Fi signal between Mars and Earth, this concept may have to wait.

FOUNDATIONS FOR THE FUTURE

The likelihood of anyone traveling to Mars is still decades—or maybe longer—away, so there's time to play around with concepts when it comes to currency. But these early ideas are laying the foundation for how people may one day pay when they're visiting the red planet.

Loose items in space can travel 10 times faster than the speed of a bullet!

CHAPTER 7

WORKING IT!

So now you know almost all there is about the past, present, and even the future of money. You know what money used to look like—and what it may look like when you're an adult. But how, exactly, do you actually earn money? Sadly, money doesn't grow on trees. And most of us won't be lucky enough to win the lottery. So making money usually starts with getting a job. In this chapter, we'll explore different kinds of jobs and ways to earn a paycheck—including some surprising jobs you may not have thought of before!

YOU'RE HIRED

EVERYTHING YOU NEED TO KNOW ABOUT BEING AN EMPLOYEE

You probably think a lot about what you want to be when you grow up: an oceanographer exploring the deepest recesses of our planet, a circus performer, an artist—or whatever else you want to be! And let's say one day you land that dream job. Regardless of how much you may make on the job (more about that on page 108!), there are certain things to know when it comes to collecting a paycheck.

PART TIME OR FULL TIME?

Usually, a job will fall into one of two categories: full time or part time. In the United States, a full-time job typically requires from 32 to 40 hours of work a week. This means a person will work about 6 to 8 hours for five days a week. Some people work many more hours than that, depending on things like how busy the job is and what its specific requirements are.

Part-time jobs, on the other hand, are those that require less than 40 hours a week. But just because someone works part-time doesn't mean they're necessarily working less: A part-time job can sometimes be just as demanding as a full-time job, and some people have more than one part-time job.

DETERMINING PAY $

How much you get paid to work depends on a bunch of things. These include your experience (the longer you've done a job or worked in a field, the more you will get paid), your education (those with college or higher degrees typically earn more), and the specific job you're doing. Jobs that require specific skills—think brain surgery or computer software writing—tend to pay more because they require more education and experience.

SALARY OR HOURLY?

Whatever your job is, if it is a full-time position, you will likely receive a salary. A salary is a fixed rate of pay which you agree to when you are hired, and you will receive a portion of that rate every month or every other week—aka payday!

So, let's say you are hired as a coder with a salary of $70,000 a year. Payday is every other Friday, or once every two weeks. Let's say there are 52 Fridays in a year, and you will be paid on half of them, or 26 Fridays. So you'd divide $70,000 by 26 to come up with your "gross pay" of $2,692. (Gross pay is the total amount of money you get before taxes or other deductions are subtracted from your salary; see "The Government's Cut" sidebar for more info on this.)

On the other hand, if you are a part-time employee, you are likely going to be paid hourly. This means you will make a certain amount of money—or wages—for every hour you work. Many first-time jobs, such as babysitting, dog walking, or newspaper delivery, are paid by the hour.

Let's say you're hired to babysit your neighbors' toddler at a rate of $10 an hour. If you babysit for four hours, they will pay you $40.

YESSS!!!

THE GOVERNMENT'S CUT

>> When it comes to a salary, the amount of money you take home from your job (your "net" pay) is going to be less than the amount of your salary (your "gross" pay) because some of your income goes to the government. The money that is taken out of your check helps pay for things like schools, roads, and even the salaries of teachers and police officers. In the United States, these are known as required deductions, meaning that they have to happen by law.

Here are some of the required deductions in the United States that you'll likely see on a future paycheck:

FEDERAL INCOME TAX: Funds that support public services, such as improving education and public transportation and providing disaster relief.

SOCIAL SECURITY TAXES: Provides benefits for retired workers and support for families of workers who have passed away.

MEDICARE TAX: Provides health coverage to people who are over 65 or have disabilities.

105

FIVE FAST FACTS ABOUT
MINIMUM
WAGE

How much will you make when you start to work? It depends on the job, of course, but by law, you should make at least the minimum wage—or the lowest hourly amount an employer may pay an employee. While minimum wage isn't required around the world, many countries offer it at a rate that is based on the nation's economy and cost of living. Here's more to know about minimum wage.

1

In 1894, New Zealand became the first nation in the world to set a minimum wage for workers. The Australian state of Victoria followed in 1896, and then the U.K. in 1909.

2

A minimum wage was first introduced in the United States during the Great Depression under President Franklin Delano Roosevelt as part of the Fair Labor Standards Act of 1938. Meant to protect people from working too much and making too little, the minimum wage at the time was set to just 25 cents an hour (which would be about five dollars an hour today).

I KNOW 3 TRADES
I SPEAK 3 LANGUAGES
FOUGHT FOR 3 YEARS
HAVE 3 CHILDREN
AND NO WORK FOR
3 MONTHS
BUT I ONLY WANT
ONE JOB

WAGE WARS

>> Minimum wage has always been a hot-button topic—especially in the United States. And in recent years, many people have fought for a raise across the board. Opponents of a raise say that it may be harder for businesses to stay afloat if they have to pay their workers more, which could lead to fewer jobs and more poverty, and may ultimately hurt the economy. But supporters of an increase believe just the opposite. They hope the entire country will one day soon adopt a policy to pay workers at least $15 an hour regardless of where you call home.

3

Today, in the United States, minimum wage can be determined at the state and local levels and is determined by the area's cost of living. The pricier it is to live in a particular place, usually the higher the wage. In the U.S., those living in major cities like Washington, D.C., and New York City earn at least $15 an hour. There is also a federal minimum wage, which is the minimum amount people can earn no matter where in the country they live. Today, that amount is about $7.25 an hour.

By 2024, many McDonald's employees will make an average of $15 an hour.

5

Restaurant waiters typically earn much less than the minimum wage—currently the hourly rate is often around $2.13—because they're expected to make up the difference with tips. So don't forget to remind your parent or guardian to tip your waiter the next time you eat out!

4

Geneva, Switzerland, offers one of the highest minimum wages at 23 Swiss francs (or about $25 [U.S.]) an hour.

Note: All statistics are from the time of this book's publication.

Guest Check

CHECK NUMBER 905805

SERVER | TABLE | GUESTS

Coffee

toast

WHO MAKES WHAT?

Ever wonder how much you'd be paid if you were the president of the United States? What about a veterinarian? Here's a look at the salaries of some of the highest-paying jobs around.*

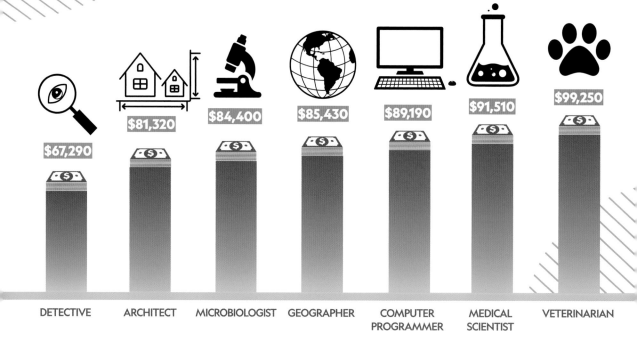

DETECTIVE	ARCHITECT	MICROBIOLOGIST	GEOGRAPHER	COMPUTER PROGRAMMER	MEDICAL SCIENTIST	VETERINARIAN
$67,290	$81,320	$84,400	$85,430	$89,190	$91,510	$99,250

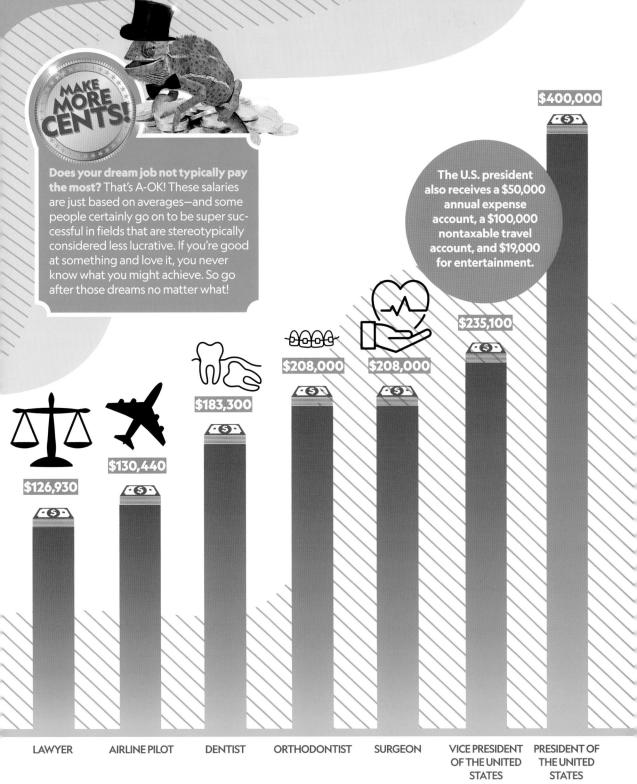

MAKE MORE CENTS!

Does your dream job not typically pay the most? That's A-OK! These salaries are just based on averages—and some people certainly go on to be super successful in fields that are stereotypically considered less lucrative. If you're good at something and love it, you never know what you might achieve. So go after those dreams no matter what!

The U.S. president also receives a $50,000 annual expense account, a $100,000 nontaxable travel account, and $19,000 for entertainment.

$400,000

$235,100

$208,000

$208,000

$183,300

$130,440

$126,930

LAWYER

AIRLINE PILOT

DENTIST

ORTHODONTIST

SURGEON

VICE PRESIDENT OF THE UNITED STATES

PRESIDENT OF THE UNITED STATES

*Numbers are estimates based on median salaries in the United States in 2020 and are sourced from the U.S. Bureau of Labor Statistics.

FAMOUS FIRST JOBS

You've got to start somewhere! Before they made the big bucks—or made history—these extraordinary people had pretty, well, ordinary jobs. Even better? They used some of their earnings to give back to others in need. Sweet!

THE PERSON: Robert L. Johnson
THE JOB: Newspaper delivery person
THE STORY: Before he became the first African American billionaire, Johnson had a paper route in his hometown of Freeport, Illinois. But he says he didn't like the early-morning hours, and he wound up dumping the papers in the trash!
HOW HE GIVES BACK: With a $30 million donation, Johnson established a fund to help Liberian entrepreneurs go after their business dreams. He's also donated priceless pieces of art from his private collection to the Smithsonian National Museum of African American History and Culture.

THE PERSON: Alexander Hamilton
THE JOB: Shipping clerk
THE STORY: As an orphan living on the Caribbean island of St. Croix, the Founding Father worked at a shipping port before immigrating to the United States, where he eventually became the first Treasury secretary of the newly formed country.
HOW HE GAVE BACK: While Hamilton died rather young (he was around 47 when he was killed in a duel), he donated to charitable causes and co-founded an organization that worked to ban slavery in New York. Later, his wife Eliza carried on his legacy by raising funds to build an orphanage.

THE PERSON: Barack Obama
THE JOB: Ice-cream scooper
THE STORY: As a teen living in Honolulu, Hawaii, Obama had a summer job scooping ice cream. Years later, he went on to become the 44th president of the United States from 2009 to 2017—and the first African American to hold the office.
HOW HE GIVES BACK: While president, Obama gave more than one million dollars to charities, mostly to groups that help children in need. Later, he donated two million dollars to the city of Chicago to help fund jobs for young people.

THE PERSON: Taylor Swift
THE JOB: Christmas tree debugger
THE STORY: Pop star Swift had a less-than-glamorous gig before earning her hundreds of millions: She knocked praying mantis pods out of Christmas trees before customers took them home from a farm in her home state of Pennsylvania, U.S.A.
HOW SHE GIVES BACK: Swift once donated some $70,000 worth of books to a library in her hometown of Reading, Pennsylvania, offered up one million dollars to help hurricane relief in Nashville, Tennessee, U.S.A., and has made several other donations to cover medical expenses for some of her fans.

THE PERSON: Oprah Winfrey
THE JOB: Checkout clerk
THE STORY: She may be worth about $2.7 billion today, but Winfrey once collected a much smaller paycheck working at a local grocery store as a teen. It wasn't long before she found broadcasting, got her own TV show, and amassed amazing wealth.
HOW SHE GIVES BACK: Known for her frequent charitable donations, Winfrey has given millions to various causes focusing on everything from public school programming to natural disaster relief. In 2020, she pledged $10 million to help feed local communities during the coronavirus pandemic.

THE PERSON: Mary Barra
THE JOB: Quality inspector
THE STORY: The first female CEO of a major U.S. automaker, Barra got her start on the assembly line at General Motors as an 18-year-old. Now worth an estimated $60 million as the boss of GM, Barra once spent hours a day looking for flaws in parts used to make cars.
HOW SHE GIVES BACK: In addition to other philanthropic activity, Barra oversaw a $255,000 donation from General Motors to Black Girls Code, a nonprofit focused on technology education for African American girls.

Want to know more about philanthropy, the act of doing something good to help others? Check out page 144 for more details about giving back!

CHANGEMAKERS

While money can go far in helping others in need, donations of personal time and effort are just as valuable. In other words, you don't have to offer up millions to make the world a better place; lending some elbow grease, brainpower, or talent to a cause can also create positive change. Here's a look at six humanitarians throughout history who have made priceless contributions in their communities and around the world—without the motivation of money.

WHO: Agatha Christie
LIVED: 1890–1976
HER STORY: Although she ultimately became famous for being a best-selling author of mystery books, Christie rolled up her sleeves as a volunteer nurse during World War I. As her husband went off to fight on the front lines, she dedicated more than 3,000 hours of time to the British Red Cross caring for wounded soldiers.

WHO: Mohamed Mashaly
LIVED: 1944–2020
HIS STORY: Known as Egypt's "Doctor of the Poor," Mashaly spent much of his career tending to the underprivileged without any interest in gaining personal wealth. Working 12-hour days, he saw up to 50 patients a day, charging them the equivalent of about 50 cents a visit.

WHO: Norman Borlaug
LIVED: 1914–2009
HIS STORY: An agricultural scientist, Borlaug developed a type of wheat plant that was less likely to get diseases and produced more than the traditional wheat plant. The result? An increase of food production around the world, ultimately saving millions of people from starvation and famine. He won the Nobel Peace Prize in 1970.

WHO: Shadrack Frimpong
LIVED: 1990–
HIS STORY: In 2017, Frimpong founded Cocoa360, a nonprofit aimed at supporting health clinics and schools in rural Ghana through funds raised in community cocoa farms. His efforts have helped thousands of patients and students in need.

WHO: Emma Watson
LIVED: 1990–
HER STORY: You may know her as Hermione in the Harry Potter movies, but Watson does plenty behind the scenes, too. As a United Nations Women's Goodwill Ambassador, she has volunteered her time on efforts to improve education and equality for girls in places like Bangladesh and Zambia.

WHO: Lupita Nyong'o
LIVED: 1983–
HER STORY: The actress and elephant lover spends time speaking up about protecting pachyderms, including advocating for the end of the illegal trade of ivory, which contributes to poaching.

WHIZ KIDS!

They may be young, but these kids used their smarts and business savvy to strike it rich with innovative ideas.

THE KID: Emil Motycka
THE BUSINESS: Emil's Lawns
DETAILS BEHIND THE DOLLARS: From mowing neighborhood lawns to making millions! Emil began mowing lawns at age eight, and by the time he was 13, he leveled up his lawn business with a commercial mower. Today, Emil's Lawns has dozens of employees and has serviced some 2,500 homes in and around Emil's hometown of Boulder, Colorado, U.S.A.

THE KID: Mikaila Ulmer
THE BUSINESS: Me and the Bees Lemonade
DETAILS BEHIND THE DOLLARS: When she was just four years old, Mikaila came up with the concept of creating a lemonade with honey bought from local beekeepers. Using her great-grandmother's recipe for flaxseed lemonade, she did just that—and has been focusing on saving the vulnerable honeybees one sip at a time. Today, a teenage Mikaila helps to oversee her company, which has sold more than a million bottles across a thousand stores in the United States and has expanded to beeswax-infused lip balms as well. Mikaila used the buzz from her business to launch the Healthy Hive, a nonprofit supporting research, education, and protection projects for honeybees.

THE KID: Moziah Bridges
THE BUSINESS: Mo's Bows
DETAILS BEHIND THE DOLLARS: At age nine, this sharply dressed kid turned his love of bow ties into a big business. What started as a project with Moziah and his grandma at her kitchen table transformed into a brand that's been featured on national TV—and has sold more than $700,000 worth of bow ties, neckties, and pocket squares. Through his bow business, Mo has rubbed elbows with famous folks like presidents Barack Obama and George W. Bush.

THE KID: Madison Greenspan
THE BUSINESS: Maddie Rae's Slime Glue
DETAILS BEHIND THE DOLLARS: At age 12, while making slime at home, Maddie came up with an idea that really, well, stuck: a special formula of glue made especially for slime. With the help of her dad, who owns a company that makes housewares and toys, Maddie bottled up the glue and began to sell it online. The glue took off and soon began selling worldwide. Eventually, Maddie's business expanded to slimemaking accessories including containers, coloring, and charms. Maddie even set a Guinness World Record when she led hundreds of kids in making a whopping 13,820 pounds (6,269 kg) of slime at a convention in 2017.

In the United States, you aren't legally allowed to work until the age of 14, with special exceptions for certain jobs. (The rules for gigs where you're doing a service for an individual instead of a company, like babysitting or dog walking, are set by the person hiring you, not the law, so you can start those at any age.) But some kids and teens with big ideas get a jump start on jobs—and success.

ODD
JOBS

WILD AND WACKY WAYS TO MAKE A BUCK!

EAT AND **EARN**

Ever wish you could get paid to *eat*? Professional eaters make a living doing just that. But this is no conventional consumption: Whether it's downing hot dogs at a rate of seven a minute or stuffing their pieholes with an entire pie in 32 seconds, pro eaters go to the extreme—and then some. **PAYDAY:** A winner of a major eating competition can walk away with $10,000 after a single event, but some of the stars in the field can collect $500,000 or more in a year in winnings and sponsorship deals.

PLAY AND GET PAID

Talk about a dream job! Professional video gamers make bank by, well, playing video games. Tournaments showcasing their gaming skills—where they win prize money based on beating levels—have pro players going head-to-head (or remote-to-remote). **PAYDAY:** Major video game championships offer some $100,000 to the winner. But the most popular players can make millions more through sponsorship and endorsement deals.

OUT OF THE BOX

Influencers are everywhere online these days—and many of them collect major profit with every post. Take unboxers, for example. Simply by revealing and reviewing new toys and other items and posting them on their social media channels, some unboxers make unbelievable amounts of money.

PAYDAY: Popular unboxers can earn hundreds of thousands to millions a year, thanks to a huge following and ad revenue on their social media channels. (Not to mention all of the free stuff they get sent to review!)

THE WHOLE TOOTH

What do you do when your dog gets a toothache? Take her to an animal dentist, of course! These specially trained veterinarians take care of all animals' teeth, whether it's treating certain dental diseases, pulling teeth, or polishing their pearly whites. Bye-bye, doggy breath!

PAYDAY: The average salary for veterinary dentists in the United States is about $85,000—but they may make more than $100,000 depending on experience.

DIVE IN

Forget hunting for buried treasure: Golf ball divers search for lost golf balls! These scuba divers spend up to 10 hours a day plucking thousands of balls from ponds on golf courses, and they often risk running into alligators, snakes, and other animals while underwater. What do they do with the found balls? They're eventually sold to golf ball refurbishers, who fix them up and resell them—supporting the multimillion-dollar used golf ball business.

PAYDAY: Depending on the course, divers can earn about $200 a day. One diver in Florida, U.S.A., reportedly earned $15 million during his diving career by selling more than one million balls each year.

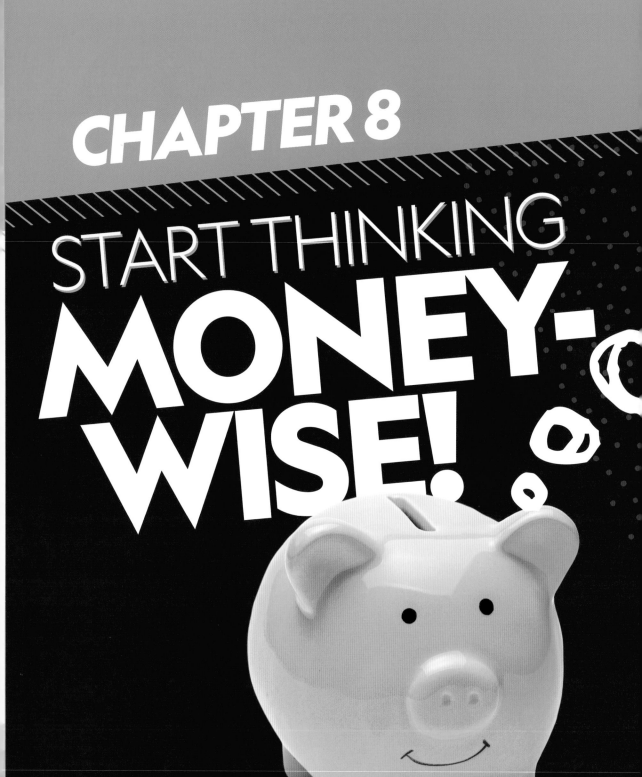

CHAPTER 8

START THINKING MONEY-WISE!

Whether you're eyeing an awesome new game, or you have dreams of one day making a big donation to your favorite cause, it's never too early to learn how to make your money grow. And that's what this chapter is all about! Read on to find out how to multiply your money starting now, whether it's by saving up those birthday bucks, earning income the old-fashioned way, or cashing in on a really great idea. But no matter how you end up earning your money, it all starts with budgeting right and spending smart. Let's go!

SAVE IT!

DIFFERENT WAYS TO STASH YOUR CASH

Sure, it's easy to run out and buy the first toy you see on the shelf or the coolest gadget of the moment as soon as you've got money in your hands. But before you buy, ask yourself: *Do I really need this?* You probably don't—and there may be something even shinier and cooler to come along in a few months or even weeks that will replace whatever it is you want right now. But that's not to say that you can't reward yourself once in a while. You just don't need to spend *all* of your savings on just a few things.

So, instead of splurging, it's smart to stash that cash for something better that comes along—or something you may actually need down the road. And you can do just that by using one of three different methods.

SAVING OPTION 1: FEED YOUR PIGGY BANK

Piggy banks may be old school, but there's a reason they've been around for centuries: Because they work! Though simple, keeping your money inside a locked (or at least sealed) container is a solid way to save.

THE PROS: You'll be able to keep a close eye on your savings and count it whenever you want. And it's motivating to save more when you see that money really start to pile up.

THE CONS: You run the risk of losing your bank or the money inside or *(gasp!)* having it swiped by a sticky-fingered sibling if you don't keep it locked up or hidden well enough. Plus, if it's right there, it's more tempting to take it out when you feel an urge to spend.

SAVING OPTION 2: PUT IT IN AN ACTUAL BANK

While most banks require you to be 18 years old to open an account, your parents can start one in your name, and you'll gain ownership of it once you're old enough.

THE PROS: You'll know your money is generally super safe in a bank, and, depending on the type of account you've set up, you may be able to earn interest (see the "Isn't It Interesting?" sidebar for more details on that!).

THE CONS: You typically can't touch your money unless your parents say it's okay. And, if they're eager for you to save up for something big, that may not happen for a very long time.

SAVING OPTION 3: INVEST IT

Again, this is something you'll need your parent or guardian's help and permission with. But with the right research and strategy, investing your money in the stock market can be a smart and simple way to save.

THE PROS: Long-term potential returns (or what you can make) are greater.

THE CONS: Because stock prices go up and down daily as a result of outside factors, the investment can be risky. But it *should* be worth the risk if the value of your investment increases.

>> The best thing about setting up a savings account? You can earn interest on your money! Interest is a little bit of extra money that the bank pays *you* each month for keeping your money with them. The interest amount isn't that much—you'll probably earn less than one percent interest each month depending on where you bank and the type of account your parents set up. But the longer you keep your savings in the account without spending it and the more you add to your account, the more your interest will grow. Which means you're basically getting free money. And what's cooler than that?

SAVINGS HACKS

Does saving the big bucks seem like an impossible task? It doesn't have to be! Here are five tips and tricks to help you grow your savings ... *stat!*

1. SEE CLEARLY.

To really *see* your savings, chuck your bucks and change into a clear jar. That way, you can watch the money grow, which can be much more motivating than shaking a piggy bank and wondering how much is in there.

2. SPEND SOME, SAVE SOME.

You don't have to put every last penny away for months. Take two jars and label one "spend" and the other "save." Whenever you have some spare change or birthday money, throw at least half of it in the "save" bank, and the rest in the other. You'll still have some spending money to play with while keeping some savings intact. If you want to take your savings smarts a step further, add a third jar and label it "give" so you can save up for a donation to a cause that's important to you.

Sixty-one percent of teens in the United States have started saving and storing their money in a bank account, according to a recent survey.

Give

Spend

Save

3. GOAL FOR IT.

What's that one big thing you *really, really* want or need? Pick one big-ticket item as your goal to save for. It'll be easier to put your money away if you have a specific purpose.

4. TIME IS RIGHT.

Then, to stay focused on saving for your goal, write down the amount of money you'll need and set a date for when you want it. Circle that date on your calendar, or write the goal on a sticky note and post it by your bed so it's the first thing you see when you go to bed and when you wake up.

MAKE MORE CENTS!

5. SHARE WITH OTHERS.

Tell people about your goal, too. The more you put your goal out there, the more likely you are to reach it. And the more others might be willing to lend a hand to help you!

The number one thing to remember when it comes to saving? Be patient! As hard as it is to resist dipping into your stash of cash, try not to touch it unless you really have to. That way, when something unexpected occurs or you're presented with an amazing opportunity that costs money, you may be really happy you spent your time saving instead of spending!

THE INS AND OUTS OF ALLOWANCE

MORE ABOUT MAKING MONEY RIGHT AT HOME

Can you get paid for just being a kid? Well, kind of. Some parents choose to pay their children a set amount of money every week or month—aka an allowance. How much you earn (and the way in which you earn it) varies from house to house, but across the board, it has remained a popular tool for teaching kids about the value of money.

"JUST BECAUSE" MONEY

The concept of allowance first went mainstream more than a hundred years ago. In fact, way back in 1912, a German parenting pro named Sidonie Matsner Gruenberg is credited for popularizing the concept in her book *Your Child Today and Tomorrow.* In it, she wrote that parents should give kids money—just as they would be given clothes and food—to experience the joy of spending and the benefits of saving. Basically, Gruenberg felt that kids deserve an allowance simply for being members of the household, not for making their beds every morning or getting straight A's on their report card. Pretty cool, huh?

EARNING IT

Gruenberg may have been on to something, but eventually parents and guardians began setting their own standards for allowance. And, according to a recent survey by the American Institute of Certified Public Accountants, more than four in five parents believe kids should receive an allowance—but they also expect them to earn it, such as by completing a chore chart. Or an allowance may be based on behavior: Did you fight with your big brother or talk back to your teacher? No money for you. Whatever the motive, it remains a popular concept: The same study showed that some 66 percent of parents in the United States give their child an allowance.

have fun

If you do get an allowance—or at least hope to one day—what should you expect to earn? Again, that's a personal choice made by your parents or guardian, so have a chat with your adults about their expectations and what they think may be a fair amount. And don't forget to ask about interest: Collecting an allowance from your parents is a great way to practice smart savings, so see if you can earn a little extra by socking most of your money away. And if your parents aren't all about that allowance? No worries! **Flip to page 132 to find out how you can start earning money in other ways.**

127

Make a Monthly Budget!

Just because you're a kid doesn't mean you can't make a plan for using your money. Here's how!

Budgeting is an important tool for keeping track of your spending, savings, and giving (who you want to donate any money to). While there are various apps and online tools to help you make a budget, you can also go old school and write it all down. Here's how to set up a basic budget for each month.

MAKE MORE CENTS!

By having a plan mapped out each month, you're more likely to stick to it—and save more! And more savings = more fun.

My Budget

MONTH:

<u>What I'm Saving For</u>: Write down your goal item: a video game, a new toy, etc.
<u>What I'll Spend On</u>: Write down any potential things you'll spend money on this month: a birthday gift for mom, ice cream with your friends, etc.

Earning Expectations
(Write down everything you think you'll earn this month.)
Allowance: $30
Gifts: $10
Odd jobs around the house: $20

Total: $60

Spending Expectations
(Write down everything you think you'll spend money on this month.)
Food and fun: $15
Toys: $5
Gifts: $20

Total: $40

Savings Expectations
(Subtract your spending from your earnings.)
$20

Make a Plan!
Decide how you will divide up that savings.
Example:
$10 to a new bicycle
$10 into my piggy bank for long-term savings

SAVINGS CHALLENGES: SHOW ME THE MONEY!

SIMPLE WAYS TO START SAVING NOW

All savings have to start somewhere. And even if you don't have much (or any!) money to your name right now, consistently setting aside some spare change now could actually turn into significant savings in the future. All you really need is a penny. Try either of these challenges to start building that stash of cash ... today!

CHALLENGE 1: FIND A PENNY

THE HOW-TO: Grab a jar or a piggy bank and toss a penny in it. The next day, add two pennies. On day three, add three pennies, then four pennies on day four, five pennies on day five, and so on. Keep this up for an entire year until you're up to adding $3.65 for day 365. If you don't touch the money all year long, you'll be $667.95 richer by the end!

TIP: Would you rather have some spending money sooner than later? Try to make it for six months. By then, you'll have $164.71 stashed away. Not too shabby.

GROWTH

CHALLENGE 2: DIVIDE AND CONQUER

THE HOW-TO: Pick a savings goal, and a date on which you'd like to hit that goal. Then, divide the money goal by the days you have to reach it. So, if you want to save $50 to buy a pair of Heelys shoes in three months, you'd divide $50 by 90 days to get $0.56 (make sure to round up!). That means you will need to save 56 cents a day. By day 90, you'll have that $50 and a bit of change to spare. Easy, right?

TIP: Share your goal with your family and friends. By putting your goal out there, you'll be more motivated to make money. (And an encouraging friend or relative might offer you a job or chore to help you earn some extra money that you can put toward your goal!)

MAKE THAT MONEY!

Just because you're a kid doesn't mean you can't start earning now.

Now that you know how to save and budget right, it's time to start earning some income with these four first jobs. Bonus: Most of the time you don't even have to leave your neighborhood!

THE GIG: PET SITTING

Next-door neighbors going on a weeklong vacation? Offer to check in on Bubbles the fish and Charlie the cat while they're away. Not only will you get extra time with some precious pets, but you'll show just how trustworthy you are.

LEVEL UP: Offer other assistance to your client, like getting the mail, watering their plants, or taking out the trash. You may score a bit more money—and if not, at least you're demonstrating that you're motivated, responsible, and worthy of a word-of-mouth recommendation.

THE GIG: PARENTS' HELPER

If you love little kids, this job's for you. You'll hang out with kids, offering an extra hand to parents and helping keep the kids safe and out of trouble. Typically, this job involves playing with toys, crafting, or building forts ... and you call this *work*?

LEVEL UP: Bring your own fun! Impress your client (and show initiative) by bringing a tote bag stocked with dollar-store crafts and library books to share with your charges.

132

THE GIG:
A LEMONADE STAND

Kids have been setting up lemonade stands since, well, people began sipping the sweet stuff. All you need is the obvious supplies (lemons, water, sugar, cups, and a table), a prime location that is in a safe and familiar neighborhood, and a knack for sweet-talking people into buying your product—and you're in business. Make sure you get a parent's or guardian's permission, too!

LEVEL UP: Get creative with your presentation! Add a twirled bit of lemon rind into each cup for added flair. Or bake up some delicious cookies and, for just a little bit extra, offer a sweet pairing with your customer's lemonade.

MAKE MORE CENTS!

When it comes to advertising your services, posting flyers around the neighborhood (with a guardian's permission) is a good start. But asking a guardian to post your offer and info on social media or a neighborhood network will get you far more reach. Just be sure to have a guardian field any replies you get: Since repliers will likely be strangers, it's important to have an adult make the arrangements or at least oversee any correspondence you have with potential customers. And if you do pass out flyers? Make sure you don't include any of your personal information: List your parents' phone number or email address instead (again, only with their okay!).

THE GIG:
YARD CLEANUP

You may not be old enough to mow the lawn, but that can't stop you from helping to beautify your yard (or your neighbor's). Pulling weeds in the spring and summer, raking and bagging leaves in the fall, and shoveling driveways in the snowy winter will keep you busy year-round!

LEVEL UP: Talk to your client about scheduling yard maintenance every other week or once a month. There's likely always going to be some work for you to do (especially in the spring, summer, and fall), and having a steady gig is great.

133

CHAPTER 9

MORE MONEY FUN!

Can't get enough details about dollars and cents? From stats on spending to unbelievable urban legends, read on to fill your brain with wow-worthy facts about finance, interesting bits about income, and other money matters. Plus, try the random savings challenge, which will help you earn a hundred dollars ... easy-peasy.

THEY SPEND WHAT?

How much people pay for everyday items each year*

Food takeout and delivery
$2,134

Halloween candy
$76

Clothes
$1,883

Electronics and gadgets
$1,480

*Values are estimates based on average annual household spending in the United States spanning the years 2015–2019 and are sourced from a composite of data sources, including the U.S. Bureau of Labor Statistics and the U.S. Public Interest Research Group.

Toys (per kid)
$482

Holiday gifts,
decor, and travel
$1,050

TV and movie
streaming
$277

Eating out
$3,536

PET SPENDING
BY THE NUMBERS

Just how much do people fork over for their furry (or not-so-furry!) friends? Find out!

Love your pet? Of course you do! So it may not be too big of a surprise that many humans spend big money to keep their animal friends happy and healthy. In fact, pet industry sales recently surpassed $100 billion in one year—a spending record in the United States that is expected to triple over the next decade. Here's more about what—and why—people pay when it comes to their pets.

70 PERCENT
of U.S. households own a pet, equal to some 90.5 million homes.

$32.3 BILLION
is spent each year on vet visits and care for all pets.

69 MILLION
of those homes own a dog; 45.3 million households have a cat (and some have both!).

$47 is the average annual price to pay for cat vitamins.

$44.1 BILLION is the total amount people spent on pet food and treats in 2021.

46 PERCENT of pet owners prefer to shop for supplies online, while 41 percent like to shop in person.

$690 is the amount the average household spends annually on pets, including food, supplies, and vet care.

$288 is the cost of a cashmere sweater made for lapdogs.

$56 is how much owners paid for dog toys a year.

A PANDEMIC PET BOOM

What's behind the boost in pet spending? Experts say the COVID-19 pandemic has a lot to do with it. While COVID brought on stress, sadness, and hardship in homes around the world, it also brought an increased demand for pets. In fact, almost 13 million households in the United States alone got an animal companion between March and December of 2020, with adoptions and purchases bringing the dog and cat population to 160 million—just about double the number from 50 years ago. And it's not just furry, four-legged friends seeing more love: Saltwater fish sales soared by 60 percent, while the purchase of birds and small animals (think hamsters and gerbils) was up by 46 percent. All told, 35 percent of pet owners say they spent more on their pet or pet supplies now than they did in years past.

New pets aren't the only ones getting a new, uh, *leash* on life after COVID. Established pets benefited from having their humans around more because of quarantine rules, virtual schooling, and work-from-home orders. One survey showed that more than half of pet owners value their pet now more than ever, and about half are more affectionate with their pets than during pre-COVID times. And because studies show that the companionship of pets can lower humans' blood pressure and reduce feelings of anxiety, loneliness, and depression, it seems like that unconditional love thing goes both ways.

MONEY MYTHS
BUSTED

Don't buy into these curious claims and tall tales!

THE MYTH: A penny placed on a railroad track can derail a train.
THE TRUTH: While urban legend holds that a penny on a railroad track has caused trains to career off the rails, there's actually no record of this ever happening. Because each freight train car weighs some 100 tons (91 t) they would likely roll right over the tiny penny.

THE MYTH: Folding a $5 bill in a specific pattern will reveal a secret image of a stack of pancakes.
THE TRUTH: After a meme went viral showing a $5 bill folded just so to reveal a stack of pancakes, people all over the country began to try their hand to complete the same feat. But experts say that no matter how you fold the bill, it will reveal no such image—and that the viral meme was just a Photoshopped hoax.

THE MYTH: If your money is ripped, it's worthless.
THE TRUTH: If your cash is damaged, don't stress. It's still worth its face value—as long as it's in decent shape. If you tore it and have the pieces, tape them back together and take it to the bank to have it exchanged for a fresh bill. As for that nearly destroyed dollar? The Bureau of Engraving and Printing Mutilated Currency Division will replace it as long as half of the bill is intact.

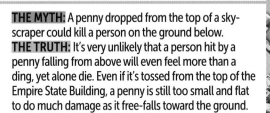

THE MYTH: A penny dropped from the top of a sky-scraper could kill a person on the ground below.
THE TRUTH: It's very unlikely that a person hit by a penny falling from above will even feel more than a ding, yet alone die. Even if it's tossed from the top of the Empire State Building, a penny is still too small and flat to do much damage as it free-falls toward the ground.

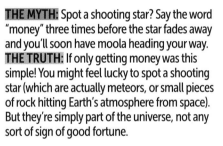

THE MYTH: Spot a shooting star? Say the word "money" three times before the star fades away and you'll soon have moola heading your way.
THE TRUTH: If only getting money was this simple! You might feel lucky to spot a shooting star (which are actually meteors, or small pieces of rock hitting Earth's atmosphere from space). But they're simply part of the universe, not any sort of sign of good fortune.

THE MYTH: Never pick up a "tails" coin from the ground, unless you want bad luck.
THE TRUTH: This belief dates back to ancient times when many cultures considered coins a precious gift from the gods—with one side representing good, and the other evil. But we now know there's no lucky or unlucky side to a coin. In fact, if you find any money on the ground, consider yourself lucky—and a few cents richer.

THE DIRTY TRUTH

>> Here's a fact we wish was a myth: Money can make you sick! Because cash and change are handled and exchanged by so many people, they're known to be germy. Thanks to its soft surface, paper money is especially rife with icky stuff, which can live for about 48 hours—or more. One study showed that the virus that causes COVID-19 can remain on paper currency for days. Your best bet to stay healthy after handling money? Wash your hands every time you touch the stuff.

141

Weird but true!

Facts About Money

Wow your friends and fam with these rich tidbits.

IT TOOK A U.S. MAN **SEVEN HOURS** TO **STACK** MORE THAN **3,000 COINS—** SOME **600 QUARTERS, 501 DIMES, 313 NICKELS, 1,700 PENNIES,** AND **5 FOREIGN COINS—ON** TOP OF A **SINGLE DIME.**

THE SHIMMERING IRIDESCENCE ON TROPICAL BUTTERFLY WINGS INSPIRED THE ANTI-COUNTERFEIT WINDOW SEEN ON SOME BANKNOTES.

In 1685, soldiers in Quebec, Canada, were **paid in playing cards** after the French colonial government **ran out of money.**

During the Middle Ages, people could pay off a debt with a button—then seen as a sign of wealth.

A farmer in Delaware **mulches** some **FOUR TONS** (3.6 t) of **worn-out U.S. cash** discarded by the U.S. Mint **into compost EVERY DAY.**

IF YOU PILED TOGETHER **ALL OF THE U.S. DOLLAR BILLS FLOATING AROUND THE WORLD,** THEY'D WEIGH AS MUCH AS 850 SCHOOL BUSES.

STOP

In Norway, **BUTTER** was once accepted as **CURRENCY** for trading.

Before 1945, the U.S. government issued **$500, $1,000, $5,000, $10,000** and even **$100,000 bills.**

If you **spent a dollar every second,** it would take about **32 YEARS** to spend a **billion dollars.**

143

PAYING IT FORWARD
WHY GIVING MONEY AWAY CAN MAKE YOU FEEL LIKE A MILLION BUCKS

Not everyone who's rolling in dough just sits back and watches their money pile up. Many people opt to give some (or *a lot*) of their money away. And the *really* rich sometimes offer up thousands and millions—or even billions—to places like universities, charities, nonprofit associations, or other good causes. This is called philanthropy, a practice that is rooted in helping other people, especially those who are less fortunate.

FIND YOUR CAUSE

Anyone can be a philanthropist. Even you! Sure, you may not have lots of money to hand out, but as you save up your dollars and cents, try to think about a cause that you may want to donate to. Are you passionate about rescue pets? Your local humane society or rescue group would be happy to take a donation of any amount. Concerned about endangered animals? Look up a nonprofit organization focused on protecting wildlife. You can even start up a fundraiser for a charity and ask your friends and family to chip in for an even more generous donation. While it may be tough to part with money, the act of paying it forward will make you feel like a million bucks.

FAMOUS PHILANTHROPISTS

Dolly Parton

DONATION DETAILS: In 2020, the country singer helped fund pharmaceutical company Moderna's COVID-19 vaccine with a $1 million donation to Vanderbilt University Medical Center in her native state of Tennessee, U.S.A.

Reed Hastings

DONATION DETAILS: In 2020, the Netflix CEO and his wife, Patty Quillin, gave $120 million to the United Negro College Fund, Spelman College, and Morehouse College to support scholarships at historically black colleges and universities.

Serena Williams

DONATION DETAILS: As one of the greatest tennis players to play the game, Williams is just as much of a star when it comes to giving back. In 2021, Williams pledged to donate more than four million face masks to underserved schools in the United States. And after winning $43,000 in a match in New Zealand in 2020, she donated all of the prize money to help wildlife relief efforts in Australia after devastating fires.

145

Money Savings Challenge!

How to start building a smart savings habit

Ready to start putting those pennies away? Try this fun savings challenge! First, work with your parent or guardian on setting a reasonable yearly savings goal. Once you have it, split up your goal into 52 tiny amounts (they don't have to all be equal!). Then, draw 52 circles on a piece of paper. Fill in the circles with the incremental amounts you came up with. (Add up the numbers again to double-check that they equal the total savings goal you set!) Each week, choose a circle at random. That's the amount you should try to save by the end of the week. Color in the bubble, and keep going until you've colored in all the bubbles. By the end of the year, you'll have met your savings goal (as long as you don't touch your savings!).

It's important to note that money flows in all our lives differently. Sometimes there are good weeks, sometimes not-so-good weeks. If you have a week where the weekly savings goal isn't possible, you can give yourself a pass if you need to. Simply draw a few more blank circles under your existing circles. For the week or weeks where you need a pass, color in one of the blank bubbles. But don't forget to start saving again the following week, if you can!

Below is an example of what a savings goal
of $50 would look like.

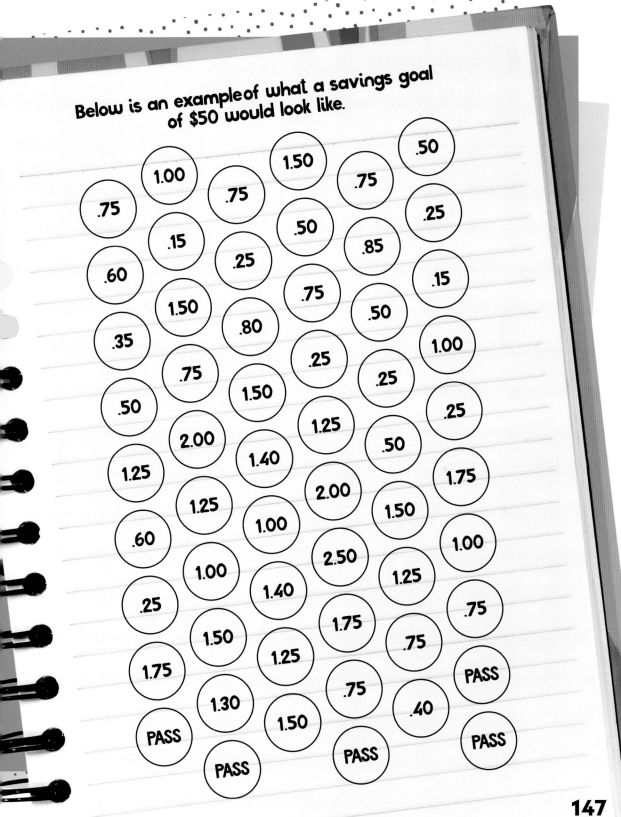

STUMP YOUR PARENTS

How much do your parents know about money? Do this quiz with them to see if their money IQ is on point—or if they need to bank a bit more knowledge. (Psst: The answers can all be found within the pages of this book.)

1. In ancient West Africa, people often traded salt for _____.
   A. squirrel pelts
   B. cows
   C. gold dust
   D. cheese

2. True or false: Nearly one in three parents admit to "borrowing" from their kid's piggy bank.

3. Early American colonists adopted the dollar sign from which currency?
   A. Bahamian dollar
   B. Chilean dollar
   C. Fijian dollar
   D. Spanish-Mexican peso

4. Fill in the blank. Expanding over an area bigger than three soccer fields, the _____ Mint covers more ground than any other mint in the world.

5. True or false: Coin collecting was once called the "hobby of all" since everyone could do it.

6. The Costa Rican colon bill features drawings of which colorful objects?
A. lemons
B. animals
C. hearts
D. unicorns

7. Experts are working on developing a currency that may be used one day on which planet?
A. Mars
B. Uranus
C. Jupiter
D. Saturn

8. True or false: Antarctica doesn't have its own form of currency.

Answers:
1. C; 2. True; 3. D; 4. Philadelphia; 5. False. It was called the "hobby of kings" because it was an expensive endeavor.; 6. B; 7. A; 8. True

GLOSSARY

ATM (automatic teller machine): A machine that dispenses money and allows customers to check their bank balance.

balance: The amount of money held in a bank account.

banknote: Any type of paper money.

barter: A way of trading goods that doesn't involve money.

blockchain: A public online log that includes transactions done with cryptocurrency.

bond: A financial product that allows an investor to loan money to a business or organization in exchange for regular interest payments.

budget: A plan for how much money you will spend and earn during a certain period.

commemorative: An adjective describing something, like a coin, that celebrates a person or event.

commodity: Objects of value that were used as early forms of currency.

compound interest: Interest on the initial amount, plus interest on prior interest. This effect grows the amount either owed or earned rapidly over time.

consumer: A person who buys a good or service.

counterfeit: Anything, including money, that's made to look real in order to cheat people.

credit card: A card that allows you to buy items using borrowed money, which you pay back later.

cryptocurrency: A type of currency that only exists online and uses digital files, or tokens, instead of physical coins or cash.

currency: Anything that is widely accepted and used as money.

debit card: A card that automatically deducts money from your account when you make a purchase.

debt: Money or other items that you owe to a person or a business.

deduction: An amount that is subtracted from a total, such as taxes from a paycheck.

employee: Someone who is hired to do a job.

employer: A person or organization who hires workers.

entrepreneur: Someone who creates his or her own business.

fiat money: Coins or banknotes that are worth more than the value of the materials they are made from.

Gold Standard: Financial system where the value of money is tied to the value of gold.

goods: Items that are made and sold to consumers.

gross domestic product (GDP): Amount of goods and services a country produces within a certain period of time, which is usually a year.

inflation: An increase in the average price of goods such as food, toys, and cars.

ingots: Rough-cut bars of silver that were the first metal used as currency.

intaglio: A design engraved or printed into a material, like coins or banknotes.

interest: The amount of money paid by people who borrow money to the people who lend it to them.

interest rate: Annual amount of interest paid on money borrowed.

investment: Placing money in a business or financial product with the hope of making more money.

loan: To lend money that must be repaid, sometimes with interest.

mint: A place where coins are made.

natural resources: Materials that are found in nature and that can be used by countries to make money or trade for other goods.

philanthropy: The act of contributing money for a good cause.

salary: A fixed amount of money paid at regular times for the work a person has done.

savings: Accumulating money or other valuable goods in a bank account or somewhere safe, such as a piggy bank.

INDEX

Boldface indicates illustrations.

A

Africa 17, **17,** 19, 77
African Americans on coins 27, **27**
Allowance 126–127, **126–127**
Animals
  on banknotes 46–47, **46–47**
  bartering 15, **15**
  as commodities 16, **16,** 17, **17**
  pet sitting 132, **132**
  pet spending 138–139, **138–139**
Antarctica 76
Anthony, Susan B. 33, **33**
Asia 77
ATM (automatic teller machine)
  cryptocurrency 96, **96**
  first 27
  futuristic bank 99, **99**
  glossary 150
  world's highest 84, **84**
Australia
  bumpy banknotes 46, **46**
  dollar 77
  kangaroo coin 19, **19,** 35, **35**
  minimum wage 106
  mint 35

B

Babylonia 13, **13,** 57
Balance
  bank accounts 59, 98
  credit cards 60
  glossary 150
  loans 59
  money market accounts 62
Banknotes *see* Paper money
Bankruptcy 66–67
Banks
  accounts for kids 59, 122–123, 124
  CDs 62
  credit cards 88
  first modern 26
  future 96–99, **98–99**
  history 57
  interest 58–59, 123
  loans 58–59
  money market accounts 62
  piggy banks 57, **57,** 122, **122,** 124, **124,** 130, **130**
  savings accounts 58–59, 80, 122–123
  types of accounts 57
  wow-worthy 84–85, **84–85**
Barnum, P. T. 67, **67**
Barra, Mary 111
Bartering 11, 12–15, **12–15,** 150
Bellamy, Edward 88, **88**
Belnick, Sean 119
BEP (Bureau of Engraving and Printing) 42–43, 140

Biggins, John 27, 88
Bills *see* Paper money
Bitcoin 92–93
Blockchain 92, 150
Bonds 62, 63, 150
Borlaug, Norman 112, **112**
Brazil 53, 76
Bridges, Moziah 115, **115**
British pound 25, **25,** 77
British two-pence coins 31
Budgeting 128–129, **128–129,** 150
Bureau of Engraving and Printing (BEP) 42–43, 140
Bush, George W. 115
Butter, as currency 143, **143**

C

Canada
  dollar 76
  firsts 27, **27**
  glow-in-the-dark coin 37, **37**
  mints 35
  soldiers paid in playing cards 142, **142**
  women on banknotes 47
Careers *see* Work
Cashless system 94–95, **94–95**
Cattle, as commodity 16, **16**
CDs (certificates of deposit) 62
Central African hoe money 19
Chase, Salmon P. 25, **25**
Cheese, as commodity 17, **17**

China
   100-yuan bill 46, **46,** 51
   cashless system 94
   counterfeit money 52
   dragon dollar 36, **36**
   futuristic bank 98–99,
      98–99
   history of money 19, 20,
      24, 41
   IMF contributions 83
   lucky money 80, **80**
   superstitions 81
   wow-worthy bank 84, **84**
   yuan 77, **77**
Christie, Agatha 112, **112**
Clegg, Gary 118
Cleopatra 33, **33**
Cleveland, Grover 46, **46**
Cohen, Ryan 119, **119**
Coinage Act (1792) 22
Coins 28–39
   changes in 22–23, **22–23**
   collecting 38–39, **38–39**
   errors 31, **31,** 38, **38**
   famous faces 32–33,
      32–33
   firsts 26, **26,** 27, **27**
   metals 20–21, **20–21**
   mints 30–31, **30–31**
   production process 30–31,
      30–31
   rare 36–37, **36–37**
   stacked 142, **142**
   supersize 18–19, **18–19**
Collectibles
   coins 38–39, **38–39**

credit cards 89
   as investment 63
   paper money 45
Commodities 16–17, **16–17,**
   150
Compound interest 59, 150
Continents 76–77, **76–77**
Costa Rican colons 46, **46**
Counterfeit money 50–53,
   50–53, 77, 142, 150
Countries
   factors in wealth 70–71
   richest 72–73, **72–73**
COVID-19 pandemic
   germs on money 141
   IMF in action 82
   pet spending 139
   philanthropy 145
   stock market crash 65
   World Bank in action 83
Cowrie shells 16
Cows, as commodity 16, **16**
Credit cards
   about 60–61, **60–61,** 150
   cashless system 94
   first 27
   mobile wallets 94
   in space 100
   timeline 88–89, **88–89**
Cryptocurrency
   about 92–93, **92–93,** 150
   inventions 96, **96,** 97, **97**
   space currency 100
Culture 80–81, **80–81**
Currency 76–77, 150

D

Dahl, Gary 118
Dare, Virginia 33
Debit cards 60, 94
Debt 60–61, 66–67, 81, 82
Deductions 104, 105, 150
Denmark 94
Desmond, Viola 47
Di Lullo, Roni 118
Diamonds 27, **27**
Dimes 23, 39
Dinosaurs 37, **37**
Disney, Walt 66, **66**
Dollar bill
   serial number 25, 43, 45
   slang terms for 19, 24
   symbols 44–45, **44–45**
   weight of 142
   weird facts 142, 143, **143**
   see also Paper money
Dollar sign 76

E

Earning money see Work
Ecuador 76
Egypt, ancient 13, **13,** 16, **16,**
   32, **33**
Electronic money transfer 27,
   27
Eliasberg, Louis E. 38
Elizabeth II, Queen (United
   Kingdom) 27, **27,** 46, **46,** 51
Employment see Work

Entrepreneurs
    crazy products 118–119,
      118–119
    glossary 151
    kids as 114–115, **114–115**
Errors on coins 31, **31**, 38, **38**
Europe 77
Exchange rate 74–75, 78–79

F

Federal Reserve 43
Fiat currency 48, 151
Flowing hair dollar 36, **36**
Ford, Gerald 22
Forgery *see* Counterfeit
  money
France
    gold reserves 49
    mint 34
    prehistoric bartering 12, **12**
    superstitions 81
Franklin, Benjamin 50, **50**, 51
Frimpong, Shadrack 113, **113**
Future of money 86–101
    banks 98–99, **98–99**
    cashless system 94–95,
      94–95
    credit card timeline 88–89,
      88–89
    cryptocurrency 92–93,
      92–93, 96, **96**, 97, **97**,
      150
    inventions 96–97, **96–97**
    past, present, and future
      prices 90–91, **90–91**
    space currency 100–101,
      100–101
    voice-based purchasing 95

G

Gaga, Lady 67, **67**
GDP (gross domestic product)
  72–73, 151
Geneva, Switzerland 107
Germany
    "cash doesn't stink" 81
    gold reserves 49
    IMF contributions 83
    wealth 73, **73**
    wow-worthy bank 85, **85**
Germs on money 141
Glow-in-the-dark coin 37, **37**
Goals 125, 131, 146
Gold
    coin with diamond 27, **27**
    eagle coins 22, **22**
    from meteors 49
    money history 20
    as precious metal 21, **21**
Gold reserves 48, 49, **49**
Gold Standard 48–49, 151
Golf ball divers 117, **117**
Government bonds 62, 63
Great Depression 14, 65, 106,
  106
Greece
    history of money 20, 57
    IMF loans 82
    weddings **80–81**, 81
Greenspan, Madison 115, **115**
Gross domestic product (GDP)
  72–73, 151
Gruenberg, Sidonie Matsner
  126
Guinea 79

H

Hall, Alvin 7, **7**
Hamilton, Alexander 57, 110
Hastings, Reed 145, **145**
History of money 10–27
    allowance 126
    banks 57
    bartering 11, 12–15, **12–15**,
      150
    big money 18–19, **18–19**
    changes in U.S. change
      22–23, **22–23**
    firsts 26–27, **26–27**
    history 57
    hot commodities 16–17,
      16–17
    metals 20–21, **20–21**
    paper money 24–25,
      24–25, 41
Humanitarians 112–113,
  112–113
Hyperinflation 48

I

Icelandic krona 47
IMF (International Monetary
  Fund) 82–83
India 24, 37, 77
Indonesia 78, 85
Inflation 48, 91, 151
Ingots 151
Intaglio 151
Interest 58–59, 123, 127, 151
International Monetary Fund
  (IMF) 82–83
Inventions 118–119, **118–119**
Investments
    glossary 151

for kids 122
stock market 63, 64–65, **64–65**
types of 62–63
Isle of Man 37
Italy
    gold reserves 49
    history of money 17, **17,** 26, 57
    mint 35
    superstitions 81

J

James, Richard 119
Japan 24, 77, 83
Jefferson, Thomas 32
Jobs *see* Work
Johnson, Robert L. 110
Juana Inés de la Cruz, Sor 47, **47**
Juettner, Emerich 53

K

Keller, Helen 33, **33**
Kenya **72–73,** 73, 81, **81**

L

Lady Gaga 67, **67**
Laos 79, 80, **80**
Lemonade stands 114, **114,** 133, **133**
Lincoln, Abraham
    bankruptcy 67, **67**
    on penny 32, 33, **33**
    Secret Service 50
    Treasury secretary 25

Lithuania 81
Loans 58–59, 151
Longacre, James Barton 23
Lydia (ancient kingdom) 20, 32

M

Madison, Dolley 33
Man, Isle of 37
Mandela, Nelson 77
Map 76–77
Mars (planet) 100–101, **100–101**
Mashaly, Mohamed 112
McDonald's 85, **85,** 107
McNamara, Frank 88
Metal money *see* Coins
Meteors 49, 141, **141**
Mexico 47, **47,** 76, 81
Micronesia 18, **18**
Middle Ages
    bartering 14, **14**
    buttons as money 142
    commodities 17
    money jars 57
Millions 78–79
Minimum wage 106–107, **106–107**
Mints
    across the globe 34–35, **34–35**
    firsts 22, 26
    glossary 151
    how coins are made 30–31, **30–31**
Money market accounts 62
Morocco 74, **74**
Motycka, Emil 114

Mutual funds 63
Myths busted 140–141, **140–141**

N

Nakamoto, Satoshi 92
Namibia 77
Native Americans 14, **14–15**
Natural resources 70, 151
New Zealand 77, 106
Nickels 23, 32
North America 76
Norway 72, **72,** 85, **85,** 143, **143**
Numismatists 38–39, **38–39**
Nyong'o, Lupita 113, **113**

O

Obama, Barack 110, **110,** 115

P

Paddington Bear 36, **36**
Pakistan 82, 84, **84**
Panama 80
Paper money 40–53
    collecting 45
    coolest bills 47
    counterfeit 50–53, **50–53,** 77, 142
    Gold Standard 48–49
    history 24–25, **24–25,** 41
    myths busted 140, **140**
    production process 42–43, **42–43**
    symbols 44–45, **44–45**
    wacky bills 46–47, **46–47**

155

Parents' helper 132
Parmesan cheese 17, **17**
Parton, Dolly 145, **145**
Pennies
    composition 23
    errors 38, **38**
    Lincoln's face 32, 33, **33**
    myths busted 140, **140,**
        141, **141**
    official name 33
    superstitions 81, **81**
Peru 52, 76
Pet sitting 132, **132**
Pet spending 138–139,
    138–139
Peter the Great, Tsar (Russia)
    26
Philanthropy
    famous philanthropists
        110–111, 145, **145**
    find your cause 144, **144**
    glossary 151
    humanitarians 112–113,
        112–113
Philippines 19, **19,** 34, 81
Phoenicians **12–13,** 13
Piggy banks 57, **57,** 122, **122,**
    124, **124,** 130, **130**
Polish weddings **80–81,** 81
Polo, Marco 24, **24**
Prehistoric bartering 12, **12**
Prices 90–91, **90–91**
Professional eaters 116, **116**

Q
Qatar 73, **73**
Quarters 23, 31, 39
Quiz 148–149, **148–149**

R
Rai stones 18, **18**
Rare coins 31, **31,** 36–37,
    36–37, 38–39, **38–39**
Resources 70, 151
Robots 96, 98–99, **98–99**
Rome, ancient 17, **17,** 20, 32
Rome, Italy 35
Roosevelt, Franklin Delano 22,
    106, **106–107**
Russia
    gold reserves 49
    history of money 17, 26, **26**
    superstitions 81

S
Sacagawea 33, **33**
Salaries
    calculating 104
    glossary 151
    highest-paying jobs
        108–109, **108–109**
    minimum wage 106–107,
        106–107
    odd jobs 116–117
    paid in playing cards 142,
        142
Salt, as commodity 17, **17**
Savings
    challenges 130–131, **130–**
        131, 146–147, **146–147**
    glossary 151
    hacks 124–125, **124–125**
    money-wise thinking
        122–123, **122–123**
    see also Banks
Savings accounts 58–59, 80,
    122–123

Shepherd-Barron, John 27
Shopping
    future 94–95, **94–95**
    past, present, and future
        prices 90–91, **90–91**
    pet spending 138–139,
        138–139
    spending on everyday
        items 136–137, **136–137**
    see also Credit cards
Shriver, Eunice Kennedy 33
Silver coins 20, 23, 39, **39**
Singapore 72, **72**
South Africa 47, **47,** 77
South America 76
Space currency 100–101,
    100–101
Spain 24
Spending see Credit cards;
    Shopping
Squirrel pelts 17, **17**
Sri Lanka 83
Stocks 63, 64–65, **64–65**
Stones, as money 18, **18**
Superstitions 81, 141
Sweden 25, 94
Swift, Taylor 111, **111**
Switzerland 107

T
Taxes 105
Tender 37
Tissaphernes (Persian noble-
    man) 32
Tools, as money 19
Trading see Bartering
Turkey 81
Tut, King (Egypt) 37, **37**

U

Uganda 53
Ukraine **80–81,** 81
Ulmer, Mikaila 114, **114**
Unboxers 117, **117**
United Kingdom
  British pound 25, **25,** 77
  cashless system 94
  counterfeit money 53
  minimum wage 106
  Paddington Bear 50-pence
    piece 36, **36**
  two-pence error coins 31
United States
  banks 57
  changes in change 22–23,
    22–23
  coin laws 32
  colonial bartering 14, **14**
  counterfeit money 50, 51,
    52, 53
  faces on coins 32–33, **33**
  firsts 26, **26,** 27, **27**
  gold reserves 48, 49
  government bonds 62, 63
  IMF contributions 82, 83
  largest bills issued 143
  minimum wage 106–107
  mints 26, 30, 34, **34**
  paper money 25, **25,**
    42–43, 46, **46,** 50, 51
  paycheck deductions 105
  power of U.S. dollar 75
  rare coins 36, **36**
  superstitions 81
  wealth 73, **73**
  work laws for kids 115

wow-worthy bank 85
see also Dollar bill; Native
  Americans
Uzbekistan 79

V

Veterinary dentists 117, **117**
Video gamers 116, **116**
Vietnam 78
Viruses on money 141

W

Washington, Booker T. 27, **27**
Washington, George 22
Watson, Emma 113, **113**
Wearables 94, **94–95,** 95, 97,
  97
Weddings **80–81,** 81
West Africa 17, **17,** 77
Western Union 27
Williams, Serena 145, **145**
Winfrey, Oprah 111, **111**
Women on money 33, **33,** 46,
  46, 47, **47**
Work 102–119
  being an employee
    104–105, **104–105**
  famous first jobs 110–111,
    110–111
  glossary 150, 151
  humanitarians 112–113,
    112–113
  jobs for kids 132–133,
    132–133
  kids with businesses
    114–115, **114–115**

minimum wage 106–107,
  106–107
salaries of highest-paying
  jobs 108–109, **108–109**
wacky jobs 116–117,
  116–117
wacky products 118–119,
  118–119
World Bank 82–83, **82–83**
World money 68–85
  by continent 76–77, **76–77**
  country economies 70–71
  culture 80–81, **80–81**
  exchange rate 74–75
  IMF 82–83
  millions 78–79
  power of U.S. dollar 75
  richest countries 72–73,
    72–73
  World Bank 82–83, **82–83**
  wow-worthy banks 84–85,
    84–85

Y

Yap (island) 18, **18**
Yardwork businesses 114, **114,**
  133, **133**

Z

Zheng Xiangchen 89
Zimbabwe 47, 48

PHOTO CREDITS

Cover: ($100 bills), Graphic design/Shutterstock; (piggy bank), 5 second Studio/Shutterstock; (quarter), Asaf Eliaso/Shutterstock; (penny), Pete Spiro/Shutterstock; (vector doodles), pio3/Shutterstock; **Back cover:** (Chameleonaire), Kuttelvaserova Stuchelova/Shutterstock; (Chameleonaire's bow tie), rangizzz/Shutterstock; (Chameleonaire's top hat), Gemenacom/Shutterstock; (Chameleonaire's pile of gold coins), teena137/Shutterstock

Front matter: 2, 5 second Studio/Shutterstock; 3, turtix/Shutterstock; 4, Billion Photos/Shutterstock; 5, GoodMood Photo/Alamy Stock Photo; 6, Robyn Mackenzie/Shutterstock; 7, Damini Moyd; 8, Sashkin/Shutterstock

Chapter 1: 10, 5 second Studio/Shutterstock; 12, Artmim/Shutterstock; 12-13, Ivan Vdovin/Alamy Stock Photo; 13 (UP LE), Volosina/Shutterstock; 13 (UP CTR), Ivaschenko Roman/Shutterstock; 13 (UP RT), Aprilphoto/Shutterstock; 14 (UP), design56/Shutterstock; 14 (LO LE), Jag_cz/Shutterstock; 14 (LO RT), Robert Clark/National Geographic Image Collection; 15 (UP LE), Andreevaee/Dreamstime; 15 (UP RT), Jausa/Shutterstock; 15 (LO), Ira Berger/Alamy Stock Photo; 16, esvetleishaya/Adobe Stock; 17 (UP), IrinaK/Shutterstock; 17 (CTR), Anna Hoychu/Shutterstock; 17 (LO), Volodymyr Shevchuk/Adobe Stock; 18, Dmitry/Adobe Stock; 19 (UP), Erik Pendzich/Shutterstock; 19 (LO), Government of the Philippines; 20 (UP), zheltobriukh/Adobe Stock; 20 (LO LE), Ilan Amihai/Alamy Stock Photo; 20 (LO RT), Gift of the American Society for the Excavation of Sardis, 1926/Metropolitan Museum of Art; 20 (vector gold bars), Maxim Cherednichenko/Shutterstock; 21 (UP), chones/Adobe Stock; 21 (LO), Eli Maier/Shutterstock; 22 (UP), National Numismatic Collection/National Museum of American History/Smithsonian Institution; 22 (LO), Tom Grundy/Alamy Stock Photo; 23 (LE), National Numismatic Collection/National Museum of American History/Smithsonian Institution; 23 (UP RT), Ivan Vdovin/Alamy Stock Photo; 23 (LO RT), Ivan Vdovin/Alamy Stock Photo; 24 (UP), De Agostini via Getty Images/Getty Images; 24 (LO), daboost/Adobe Stock; 25 (UP LE), Kenneth Graff/Adobe Stock; 25 (UP RT), National Numismatic Collection/National Museum of American History/Smithsonian Institution; 25 (CTR), Sean Gladwell /Adobe Stock; 25 (LO), National Numismatic Collection/National Museum of American History/Smithsonian Institution; 26 (UP LE), ma8/Adobe Stock; 26 (UP RT), chamillew/Adobe Stock; 26 (LO), National Numismatic Collection/National Museum of American History/Smithsonian Institution; 27 (UP LE), Hulton Archive/Getty Images; 27 (UP RT), United States Mint; 27 (CTR), United States Mint; 27 (LO), © 2022 Royal Canadian Mint. All rights reserved.

Chapter 2: 28, Robyn Mackenzie/Shutterstock; 28-29, GoodMood Photo/Alamy Stock Photo; 30 (UP), Ambient Ideas/Shutterstock; 30 (LO), Justin Sullivan/Getty Images; 31 (UP LE), Matthew Staver/Bloomberg/Getty Images; 31 (UP RT), Craig Schreiner/Wisconsin State Journal/Associated Press; 31 (CTR), Kristoffer Tripplaar/Alamy Stock Photo; 31 (LO), Matthew Staver/Bloomberg/Getty Images; 32, Bill Curtsinger/National Geographic Image Collection; 33 (UP), Tom Grundy/Adobe Stock; 33 (CTR LE), Comugnero Silvana/Adobe Stock; 33 (CTR), Alexander Mak/Adobe Stock; 33 (CTR RT), incamerastock/Alamy Stock Photo; 33 (LO LE), Kenneth Garrett/National Geographic Image Collection; 33 (LO RT), Panther Media GmbH/Alamy Stock Photo; 34, Roman Babakin/Adobe Stock; 35 (UP), Reuters/Alamy Stock Photo; 35 (CTR), VPC Coins Collection/Alamy Stock Photo; 35 (LO), Nigel/Adobe Stock; 36 (UP), CarlsPix/Shutterstock; 36 (LO LE), National Numismatic Collection/National Museum of American History/Smithsonian Institution; 36 (LO

RT), Heritage Auctions, Dallas; 37 (UP), © 2022 Royal Canadian Mint. All rights reserved.; 37 (LO), Shutterstock; 38, Heritage Auctions, Dallas; 39 (UP), Victoria Jones/PA Images via Getty Images; 39 (CTR), Bequest of Joseph H. Durkee, 1898/Metropolitan Museum of Art; 39 (LO), Zee/Alamy Stock Photo

Chapter 3: 40, David Crockett/Shutterstock; 41, Anton Kokuiev/Shutterstock; 42, ra3rn/iStockphoto/Getty Images; 42-43, schankz/Shutterstock; 43 (UP), Mint Images Limited/Alamy Stock Photo; 43 (LO LE), Lm Otero/AP/Shutterstock; 43 (LO RT), Lauren Burke/AP/Shutterstock; 44, Gennady Kulinenko/Adobe Stock; 44-45, octofocus/Adobe Stock; 45 (UP LE), Jak149/Shutterstock; 45 (UP RT), Ezume Images/Adobe Stock; 45 (CTR), Panama/Adobe Stock; 46 (UP), taffpixture/Shutterstock; 46 (CTR LE), National Numismatic Collection/National Museum of American History, Smithsonian Institution; 46 (CTR RT), jagrawut/Adobe Stock; 46 (LO), johan10/Adobe Stock; 47 (UP), Prachaya Roekdeethaweesa/Shutterstock; 47 (LO), Arkadij Schell/Adobe Stock; 48, Chris Collins/The Image Bank RF/Getty Images; 49 (UP), Zerbor/Shutterstock; 49 (LO), sunsinger/Adobe Stock; 50 (UP), samc/Alamy Stock Photo; 50 (LO), STR/AFP via Getty Images; 51 (UP), PjrStudio/Alamy Stock Photo; 51 (CTR & LO), Lori Epstein/NG Staff; 52 (UP), AGphotographer/Adobe Stock; 52 (LO), Guadalupe Pardo/Reuters; 53, Billion Photos/Shutterstock

Chapter 4: 54-55, Robyn Mackenzie/Shutterstock; 56, Zamrznuti Tonovi/Adobe Stock; 57 (vector money), AllNikArt/Shutterstock; 57 (vector rice), JJ Chamon/Shutterstock; 57, Romolo Tavani/Shutterstock; 58, Elena Schweitzer/Shutterstock; 58-59 (UP), olavs/Shutterstock; 58-59 (LO), Hurst Photo/Shutterstock; 59, DCStockPhotography/Shutterstock; 60, Oleksiy Mark/Shutterstock; 61, Prostock-studio/Adobe Stock; 62 (LE), Andrii Zastrozhnov/Adobe Stock; 62 (RT), turtix/Shutterstock; 63 (UP LE), Zoe/Adobe Stock; 63 (UP RT), Michael Burrell/Adobe Stock; 63 (CTR), Art Villone/Alamy Stock Photo; 63 (LO LE), Gabe Palmer/Alamy Stock Photo; 63 (LO RT), Todd Strand/Alamy Stock Photo; 64, Andrew Rich/RichVintage/E+Getty Images; 65 (UP), Peter Schreiber/Shutterstock; 65 (LO), Nick Starichenko/Shutterstock; 66 (UP), Ronald Grant Archive/Alamy Stock Photo; 66 (LO), Library of Congress Prints and Photographs Division; 67 (UP), Glasshouse Images/Alamy Stock Photo; 67 (LO), Edd Westmacott/Alamy Stock Photo

Chapter 5: 68, Gts/Shutterstock; 69 (UP LE), oconnelll/Shutterstock; 69 (UP RT), Prestonia/Adobe Stock; 69 (LO), David Franklin/Adobe Stock; 71 (lemonade sign), Rubberball/Getty Images; 71, Steve Debenport/SDI Productions/E+/Getty Images; 71 (vector check marks), Tartila/Adobe Stock; 71 (vector notebook), Lysenko.A/Adobe Stock; 72 (LE), Piotr Pawinski /Adobe Stock; 72 (RT), Prestonia/Adobe Stock; 72 (all flags), NG Maps; 73 (UP), Jacek Sopotnicki/Alamy Stock Photo; 73 (LO LE), Piotr Pawinski/Adobe Stock; 73 (LO RT), Frank Boston/Adobe Stock; 73 (all flags), NG Maps; 74, Georgios Tsichlis/Alamy Stock Photo; 75 (UP), PhotoStock-Israel/Photodisc/Getty Images; 75 (LO), sosiukin/Adobe Stock; 76 (UP), Illinskiy Anatoliy/Shutterstock; 76 (LO), Brenda Blossom/Adobe Stock; 77 (vector currency symbols), Haali/Shutterstock; 77 (vector currency symbols), AdresiaStock/Shutterstock; 77 (UP), thodonal/Adobe Stock; 77 (CTR), Dave Newman/Adobe Stock; 77 (LO LE), oconnelll/Shutterstock; 77 (LO RT), David Franklin/Adobe Stock; 78 (vector wifi icon), Maksim/Adobe Stock; 78 (UP), ballabeyla/Adobe Stock; 78 (LO LE), cheremuha/Adobe Stock; 78 (LO RT), ChaoticDesignStudio/Adobe Stock; 79 (UP), Sergey Golub/Adobe Stock; 79 (LO), Pixel-Shot/Adobe Stock;

80 (LE), Miindiido/Shutterstock; 80 (RT), Xinzheng/Moment RF/Getty Images; 81 (UP LE), Adam van Bunnens/Alamy Stock Photo; 81 (UP CTR), rsooll/Shutterstock; 81 (UP RT), Stuart Burford/Adobe Stock; 81 (CTR), Papik/Shutterstock; 81 (LO), Lucian Coman/Shutterstock; 82, Wim Wiskerke/Alamy Stock Photo; 83, Vlad Ivantcov/Adobe Stock; 84 (UP), Kenta Ueda/Adobe Stock; 84 (LO), Sulo Letta/Adobe Stock; 85 (UP), MartineDF/Shutterstock; 85 (LO), Norman Pogson/Alamy Stock Photo

Chapter 6: 86, Alohaflaminggo/Shutterstock; 87 (vector bitcoin), VectorCreation/Shutterstock; 88 (UP LE), Bettmann Archive/Getty Images; 88 (UP RT), World History Archive/Alamy Stock Photo; 88 (CTR), Everett Collection Historical/Alamy Stock Photo; 88 (LO), Jonathan ORourke/Alamy Stock Photo; 89 (UP), Yeamake/Adobe Stock; 89 (LO LE), Fox Photos/Hulton Archive/Getty Images; 89 (LO RT), adragan/Adobe Stock; 90 (UP), vladstar/Adobe Stock; 90 (LO), Rawpixel/Shutterstock; 91 (UP LE), Konstantinos Moraiti/Adobe Stock; 91 (UP RT), Liaurinko/Adobe Stock; 91 (CTR LE), ewapee/Adobe Stock; 91 (CTR), viperagp/Adobe Stock; 91 (CTR RT), Kaneos Media/Shutterstock; 91 (LO LE), Eivaisla/Shutterstock; 91 (LO RT), Sean Locke/Adobe Stock; 92 (vector colored currency icons), Vector Archive/Adobe Stock; 92 (LO), Lukasz Stefanski/Shutterstock; 93, Rybin Dmitriy/Adobe Stock; 94, BSIP SA/Alamy Stock Photo; 94 (vector wearable smartwatch), Jeni Rodger/Shutterstock; 94 (vector doodle smartphone), Gwens Graphic Studio/Shutterstock; 94-95, Jacob Lund/Alamy Stock Photo; 95 (vector NFC icon), officeku/Shutterstock; 95 (LO), Tim Platt /Digital Vision/Getty Images; 96, Parilov Evgeniy/Adobe Stock; 97, Trove/LAYER Design; 98, Zhou Junxiang/Imaginechina/Associated Press; 99 (BOTH), SIPA Asia via ZUMA Wire/Alamy Stock Photo; 100 (vector space icons), Shemelina/Shutterstock; 101, Mondolithic Studios

Chapter 7: 102-103, wut62/Shutterstock; 104, LanaStock/iStockphoto/Getty Images; 105 (UP), lenets_tan/Adobe Stock; 105 (LO), sturti/E+/Getty Images; 106 (LE), General Photographic Agency/Hulton Archive/Getty Images; 106 (RT), Keystone Features/Hulton Archive/Getty Images; 106-107, f11photo/Adobe Stock; 107 (UP), Bill Clark/CQ-Roll Call, Inc via Getty Images; 107 (LO), cherylvb/Adobe Stock; 108 (vector detective icon), ArtbyInez/Adobe Stock; 108 (vector architecture icon), RedlineVector/Adobe Stock; 108 (vector microbiologist icon), imdproduction/Adobe Stock; 108 (vector geographer icon), Graficriver/Adobe Stock; 108 (vector computer programmer icon), Farbai/Adobe Stock; 108 (vector medical scientist icon), Graficriver/Adobe Stock; 108 (vector veterinarian icon), Marc/Adobe Stock; 108 (vector lawyer icon), ihorzigor/Adobe Stock; 109 (vector airline pilot icon), Comauthor/Adobe Stock; 109 (vector dentist icon), nadiinko/Adobe Stock; 109 (vector orthodontist icon), nadiinko/Adobe Stock; 109 (vector surgeon icon), spiral media/Adobe Stock; 109 (vector vice president icon), Vector Tradition/Adobe Stock; 109 (vector president icon), Vector Tradition/Adobe Stock; 110 (UP), mipan /Adobe Stock; 110 (CTR), Larry Downing/Reuters; 110 (LO), aanbetta/Adobe Stock; 111 (UP LE), Dmitry Lobanov/Adobe Stock; 111 (UP RT), Kevin Kane/WireImage/Getty Images; 111 (LO), Vera Anderson/WireImage/Getty Images; 112 (UP), Hulton Archive/Getty Images; 112 (CTR), pixelrobot/Adobe Stock; 112 (LO LE), Micheline Pelletier/Sygma via Getty Images; 112 (LO RT), Nitr/Adobe Stock; 113 (UP LE), volff/Adobe Stock; 113 (UP RT), Stephen J. Cohen/Getty Images; 113 (CTR LE), Eduardo Munoz Alvarez/Getty Images; 113 (CTR RT), Elnur/Adobe Stock; 113 (LO LE), Roy Rochlin/Getty Images; 113 (LO RT), Patryk Kosmider /Adobe Stock; 114 (UP), sergiy1975/Adobe Stock; 114 (CTR), Sarah J. Mock/NG Staff; 114 (LO), Eugene Gologursky/Getty Images for

Macy's, Inc.; 115 (UP LE), Sheri Determan/WENN Rights Ltd/Alamy Stock Photo; 115 (UP RT), Giovanni Rufino/Disney General Entertainment Content/Getty Images; 115 (LO), SCS Direct, Inc.; 115 (slime), New Africa/Adobe Stock; 116 (UP), Reuters/Alamy Stock Photo; 116 (LO), Michal Konkol/Riot Games Inc. via Getty Images; 117 (UP), Antonio Guillem Fernandez/Alamy Stock Photo; 117 (CTR), boryanam/Adobe Stock; 117 (LO), imageBROKER/Shutterstock; 118 (UP), Alysta/Adobe Stock; 118 (LO), Peter Lawson/Shutterstock; 119 (UP), Richard Watkins/Alamy Stock Photo; 119 (CTR), Michael/Adobe Stock; 119 (LO), Jamel Toppin/The Forbes Collection/Contour by Getty Images

Chapter 8: 120, ADragan/Shutterstock; 121, Richard Drury/Digital Vision/Getty Images; 122 (UP), PM Images/Stone RF/Getty Images; 122 (LO), Billion Photos/Shutterstock; 123, Mmaxer/Shutterstock; 124 (UP), Roman Motizov/Adobe Stock; 124 (CTR), Steven Frame/Shutterstock; 124 (LO), Faroq/Adobe Stock; 125 (UP), Jamie Grill/Tetra images RF/Getty Images; 125 (CTR), Fevziie/Adobe Stock; 125 (LO LE), Atstock Productions/Adobe Stock; 125 (LO RT), Pixel-Shot/Adobe Stock; 126 (LE), Knape/E+/Getty Images; 126 (RT), Tom Werner/Digital Vision/Getty Images; 127, E+/Getty Images; 128, Billion Photos/Shutterstock; 129, NuEngine/Shutterstock; 130 (UP), photovs/Shutterstock; 130 (LO), Joellen L Armstrong/Shutterstock; 130-131, PM Images/Digital Vision/Getty Images; 131, IdeaBug/Adobe Stock; 132, Inti St. Clair/Stocksy; 133 (UP), maxsol7/Adobe Stock; 133 (LO), Lawrence Manning/Stocksy

Chapter 9: 134-135, Hammon Photography/Shutterstock; 136 (fast food), Soho A Studio/Shutterstock; 136 (sweatshirt), nys/Adobe Stock; 136 (Halloween candy), Jennifer Barrow/Dreamstime; 136 (electronic tablet), Denys Prykhodov/Shutterstock; 136 (baseball cap), Pixfiction/Shutterstock; 136 (jeans), Karkas/Shutterstock; 137 (passport), M.Stasy/Shutterstock; 137 (robot), charles taylor/Shutterstock; 137 (remote control), Ovydyborets/Dreamstime; 137 (taco), MaraZe/Shutterstock; 138 (UP), BG-FOTO/Shutterstock; 138 (LO), Cat'chy Images/Shutterstock; 139 (UP LE), Richard Peterson/Shutterstock; 139 (UP RT), Aldo Murillo/E+/Getty Images; 139 (CTR), Barbara Helgason/Adobe Stock; 139 (LO LE), cynoclub/Shutterstock; 139 (LO RT), BW Folsom/Shutterstock; 140 (UP LE), rtrible/iStockphoto/Getty Images; 140 (UP RT), Ivo Roospold/Alamy Stock Photo; 140 (LO), Shayan Shidfar/EyeEm/Getty Images; 141 (UP), Liyao Xie/Moment RF/Getty Images; 141 (CTR LE), Kevin Key/Slworking/Moment RF/Getty Images; 141 (CTR RT), welzevoul/Shutterstock; 141 (LO), Laurence Mouton/PhotoAlto/Getty Images; 142 (UP LE), aetb/Adobe Stock; 142 (UP RT), Sari ONeal/Shutterstock; 142 (CTR LE), Aleem Zahid Khan/Shutterstock; 142 (CTR RT), Picsfive/Shutterstock; 142 (LO), Joy Brown/Shutterstock; 143 (UP), Nalaphotos/Shutterstock; 143 (CTR), Robyn Mackenzie/Shutterstock; 143 (LO), Typhoonski/Dreamstime; 144, Jeffrey Isaac Greenberg /Alamy Stock Photo; 145 (UP LE), NBCUniversal/Getty Images; 145 (UP RT), Pierre Costabadie/Icon Sport via Getty Images; 145 (LO), Ian White Photography LLC/Contour RA via Getty Images; 146, Kellis/Shutterstock; 148, Chones/Shutterstock; 148-149, annt/Shutterstock; 149 (UP LE), Tatiana Popova/Shutterstock; 149 (UP RT), GoodMood Photo/Alamy Stock Photo; 149 (LO LE), Antony McAulay/Shutterstock; 149 (LO RT), Leksele/Shutterstock; 151, 5 second Studio/Shutterstock; (Chameleonaire's gold coin), Albert Stephen Julius/Shutterstock; (Chameleonaire's bow tie), rangizzz/Shutterstock; (Chameleonaire), Kuttelvaserova Stuchelova/Shutterstock; (Chameleonaire's top hat), Gemenacom/Shutterstock; (Chameleonaire's pile of gold coins), teena137/Shutterstock; (vector doodles), pio3/Shutterstock

159

FOR MY FAMILY, WHO ALWAYS MAKES ME FEEL RICH WITH LOVE. —SWF

Since 1888, the National Geographic Society has funded more than 14,000
research, conservation, education, and storytelling projects around the world.
National Geographic Partners distributes a portion of the funds it receives from
your purchase to National Geographic Society to support programs including the
conservation of animals and their habitats. To learn more, visit natgeo.com/info.

For more information, visit nationalgeographic.com,
call 1-877-873-6846, or write to the following address:

National Geographic Partners, LLC
1145 17th Street N.W.
Washington, DC 20036-4688 U.S.A.

For librarians and teachers: nationalgeographic.com/books/librarians-and-educators

More for kids from National Geographic: natgeokids.com

National Geographic Kids magazine inspires children to explore their world with fun
yet educational articles on animals, science, nature, and more. Using fresh storytelling
and amazing photography, *Nat Geo Kids* shows kids ages 6 to 14 the fascinating
truth about the world—and why they should care. **natgeo.com/subscribe**

For rights or permissions inquiries, please contact National Geographic Books
Subsidiary Rights: bookrights@natgeo.com

Designed by Kathryn Robbins

The publisher thanks everyone who made this book possible:
Ariane Szu-Tu, editor; Lori Epstein, photo editor; Michelle Harris, fact-checker;
Mary Wages, contributing designer; Molly Reid, production editor; Anne LeongSon
and Gus Tello, design production assistants; Larry Shea, copy editor; Gwenda Larsen,
proofreader; Ebonye Gussine Wilkins for her sensitivity review; James D. Jeffery
for his review and being the inspiration behind this book; and Alvin Hall,
author of the award-winning children's book *Show Me the Money*.